Critical Cultural Studies of Childhood

Series Editors
Marianne Bloch
Westport, WI, USA

Elizabeth Blue Swadener
School of Social Transformation
Arizona State University
Tempe, AZ, USA

This series focuses on reframings of theory, research, policy, and pedagogies in childhood. A critical cultural study of childhood is one that offers a 'prism' of possibilities for writing about power and its relationship to the cultural constructions of childhood, family, and education in broad societal, local, and global contexts. Books in the series open up new spaces for dialogue and reconceptualization based on critical theoretical and methodological framings, including critical pedagogy; advocacy and social justice perspectives; cultural, historical, and comparative studies of childhood; and post-structural, postcolonial, and/or feminist studies of childhood, family, and education. The intent of the series is to examine the relations between power, language, and what is taken as normal/abnormal, good, and natural, to understand the construction of the 'other,' difference and inclusions/exclusions that are embedded in current notions of childhood, family, educational reforms, policies, and the practices of schooling. Critical Cultural Studies of Childhood will open up dialogue about new possibilities for action and research. Single-authored as well as edited volumes focusing on critical studies of childhood from a variety of disciplinary and theoretical perspectives are included in the series. A particular focus is in a reimagining and critical reflection on policy and practice in early childhood, primary, and elementary education. The series intends to open up new spaces for reconceptualizing theories and traditions of research, policies, cultural reasonings, and practices at all of these levels, in the United States, as well as comparatively.

More information about this series at
http://www.palgrave.com/gp/series/14933

Victoria Flavia Namuggala

Childhood, Youth Identity, and Violence in Formerly Displaced Communities in Uganda

palgrave
macmillan

Victoria Flavia Namuggala
Makerere University
Kampala, Uganda

Critical Cultural Studies of Childhood
ISBN 978-3-030-07226-1   ISBN 978-3-319-96628-1   (eBook)
https://doi.org/10.1007/978-3-319-96628-1

© The Editor(s) (if applicable) and The Author(s) 2018
Softcover re-print of the Hardcover 1st edition 2018
This work is subject to copyright. All rights are solely and exclusively licensed by the Publisher, whether the whole or part of the material is concerned, specifically the rights of translation, reprinting, reuse of illustrations, recitation, broadcasting, reproduction on microfilms or in any other physical way, and transmission or information storage and retrieval, electronic adaptation, computer software, or by similar or dissimilar methodology now known or hereafter developed.
The use of general descriptive names, registered names, trademarks, service marks, etc. in this publication does not imply, even in the absence of a specific statement, that such names are exempt from the relevant protective laws and regulations and therefore free for general use.
The publisher, the authors, and the editors are safe to assume that the advice and information in this book are believed to be true and accurate at the date of publication. Neither the publisher nor the authors or the editors give a warranty, express or implied, with respect to the material contained herein or for any errors or omissions that may have been made. The publisher remains neutral with regard to jurisdictional claims in published maps and institutional affiliations.

Cover image: © Peter Horree/Alamy Stock Photo

This Palgrave Macmillan imprint is published by the registered company Springer Nature Switzerland AG
The registered company address is: Gewerbestrasse 11, 6330 Cham, Switzerland

I dedicate this volume to my children Gregory, Gabriel and Gareth Katende.

Series Editors' Preface

We are delighted that this volume is a part of our series, Critical Cultural Studies of Childhood, as it powerfully decenters prevailing Western assumptions about childhood and children's life experiences and makes a powerful contribution to childhood studies and related interdisciplinary fields. Drawing on her research with youth directly affected (displaced) by the protracted civil war in Northern Uganda, Victoria Namuggala shares a rich and nuanced analysis of the lives and perspectives of young people, many of whom were captured and forced into child soldier roles. Her interviews with these young people shed light on ways in which they demonstrate both vulnerability and agency. *Childhood, Youth Identity, and Violence in Formerly Displaced Communities in Uganda* uses African feminist and indigenous epistemologies to decolonize constructions and understandings of childhood and children.

This book is organized as an interrelated set of seven essays that analyze historical Western constructions of childhood, Global South and Ugandan traditions and contemporary contexts, and the "complex intersectional nature of youthhood and its cultural relevance to formerly displaced communities and how this manifests in access to and use of humanitarian assistance". The book also examines the often contradictory roles of NGOs working with such groups and the ways in which young mothers negotiate their roles as motherhood defines them as more adult.

As series co-editors and longtime colleagues doing work in sub-Saharan Africa for over three decades, we (as series editors) appreciated the depth of cultural and scholarly insights that underscore deep tensions that occur when children return, or are repatriated, at times as young parents, to their rural communities are not necessarily welcomed home. Victoria Namuggala, a scholar in Women and Gender Studies and Childhood Studies at Makerere University, negotiates her roles as an "insider outsider". Her use of youth voice and gender studies expertise is powerful, including her framing of childhood as a human right, exploring ways in which armed violence denies such rights, and limitations to using numeric age in categorizing structural inequalities affecting the girl child and female youth. From trauma to intersectional identities and contested childhood, the essays in this book will inform, inspire, and raise even more questions and contestations of ways in which childhood is typically defined and experienced.

This volume brings to our attention issues faced by many in war-torn parts of the world that are often ignored in Western-centric studies of gender and childhoods. It is urgent that we bring this work into the center of scholarship and recognize that ignorance of such events makes us complicit with persistent violence in children's lives. We urge more scholars to share work that educates us on the intersectional worlds of children in dangerous spaces, experiencing complicated childhoods.

Westport, USA   Marianne Bloch
Tempe, USA   Elizabeth Blue Swadener

Preface

The essays in this volume provide a critical assessment of mainstream Western childhood notions and their impact on the developing world. Using African feminist and indigenous epistemological frameworks, this volume seeks to decolonize the understanding of childhood and children. This volume consists of seven essays, which are thematically connected, yet can as well stand as independent chapters. The essays discuss a number of issues including the historical construction of childhood, and the use of numeric age in categorizing population and structural inequalities affecting the girl child and the female youth. The essays additionally explore a number of issues regarding Westernization, (Ugandan) traditions, individual and collective identities and sense of belonging. Specifically, the volume presents Global South contestations of mainstream Western constructions exploring alternative notions to childhood. The essays critique and problematize some prevalent notions related to culture, identity, and vulnerability and belonging especially in situations of armed violence. The volume also deliberates childhood as a human right exploring how armed violence hinders realization of such rights focusing on humanitarian assistance programs implemented in northern Uganda. Besides childhood, this book also explores the complex intersectional nature of youthhood and its cultural relevance to formerly displaced communities and how this manifests in access to and use of humanitarian assistance. In conclusion, the volume acknowledges the agency and resilience of young people despite the numerous challenges and traumas they encounter especially during situations of forced displacement.

This volume also brings together both Western and Global South approaches to childhood. In other words, it is an intersection of these two, and their complex dynamics. The book is interdisciplinary, drawing on childhood studies, peace and conflict studies, cultural studies, and feminist studies. It offers descriptive material from a place and people not often included in discussions of the development and lives of children and youth but reflective of other places and conditions outside Uganda and Africa. The volume thus positions African/Ugandan childhoods within mainstream childhood standards.

Kampala, Uganda   Victoria Flavia Namuggala

Acknowledgements

I wholeheartedly thank the youth and the key informants who accepted to share their time and insights and take part in this study amidst challenging survival circumstances. I hope this volume represents most of the complexities engulfed in their daily lives.

I owe my appreciation to many people who have read through the various versions of the essays presented in this book. They all gave me helpful comments as well as criticisms. Colleagues at the School of Women and Gender Studies, Makerere University were equally supportive.

I also received helpful comments from people outside my workplace. I thank my doctoral committee members—Dr. Karen Leong and Dr. Lisa Anderson at Arizona State University. A special thank you goes to Prof. Beth Blue Swadener for reading through the chapter drafts, creating opportunities to meet and discuss with other researchers and scholars in the field of childhood studies, as well as continual encouragement.

I am forever indebted to my family—children, partner, brothers, and sisters for the unceasing support. Finally, I am grateful to my dear parents—Engineer Gerald Lukwago and Angel Nalubega. While they have not lived long enough to see this book released, they are a great contribution to who and what I am. They believed in me as a person but also highly prioritized girl-child education.

Contents

1 **Introduction**   1
   Reference   4

2 **Overview: Childhood and Armed Violence**   5
   Childhood Amidst Armed Conflict and Displacement   7
   Global Discourses on Internal Displacement   8
   Brief Overview of Global Armed Violence   11
   Armed Conflict and Forced Internal Displacement in Africa   12
   Uganda's Political Contention and the LRA Insurgency in Northern Uganda   14
   The Impact of Dominant Western Frameworks on Global South Childhoods   18
   Feminism and Armed Violence   19
   References   22

3 **The Construction of Childhood**   27
   Introduction   27
   Historical Overview to Dominant Notions of Childhood   28
   The Right to Childhood   31
   Childhood in Africa   42
   Government of Uganda's Perspective on Childhood   44
   Conclusion   46
   References   47

4 Local Perceptions of Childhood, Youthhood, and Adulthood   51
Introduction   51
Reframing Knowledge from an African Perspective   52
Contextualizing Childhood in Northern Uganda   54
Contradictions Between Mainstream Western and Local Indigenous Constructions of Childhood   56
Shifting Safety Zones   63
Intersectionality and Childhood   64
Child Laboring for Survival   66
Reframing Young People's Vulnerability   69
Pre-conflict versus Post-conflict Childhood in Northern Uganda   72
Conclusion   75
References   77

5 We Are What We Are Not   81
Introduction   81
Cultural Relevance of the Concept Youth   83
Education, Choice, and Identity   88
Youthhood as a Contributor to Violence   92
Feminist Critiques to the Youth Bulge Theory   94
Conclusion   103
References   103

6 Girlhood, Violence, and Humanitarian Assistance   107
Introduction   107
Overview and Understanding of Humanitarian Assistance   109
Uganda and Humanitarian Assistance   111
The Nature of Assistance Provided to Returning Populations   113
Girlhood and Violence   118
Government Efforts to Combat Violence Against Women and Girls   119
Post-conflict Conditions Contributing to Violence Against Young Women   120
Conclusion   133
References   134

7	**Young People's Agency and Resilience**	139
	Introduction	139
	Contextualizing Resilience and Agency	140
	Young Peoples' Experiences and Strategies During Displacement	141
	Youth Experiences and Strategies in Areas of Return	147
	Challenging Victimization	148
	References	156
8	**Conclusion and Recommendations**	157
	Institutional and Structural Approaches	163
	Final Word	165
	References	166
Index		169

Author's Positionality

The concept "child or children" sounds a very familiar one to almost everyone. It is something that we all think we know yet it is as complex and diverse as situations and lived realities there are in the world. This book is a result of my doctoral dissertation research conducted in northeastern Uganda. The impetus to do this research, however, was informed by my difficulty to situate my childhood experiences in the normative/ dominant understandings we often discussed in the classrooms. As a child born, raised, and educated in Uganda (East Africa), it was clear, given my experience, what the United Nations Convention Rights of the Child (UNCRC) stipulated relating to childhood including protection, education, and participation could not be actualized in the lives of many children in Uganda. It is even worse for children residing in areas affected by armed conflict, a situation that characterized much of post-independence Uganda and northern Uganda for over two decades. Children in situations of violence and displacement are multiply disadvantaged and marginalized yet at the same time agentic and resilient. Such intersecting yet contradictory childhood narratives are not acknowledged in dominant childhood narratives, which emphasize protection, participation, and provision for the children. As I read articles and books on childhood, the more apparent it became that the understanding of vulnerability, protection, child labor, child abuse, and child marriages among other conceptualizations were in most cases conceptualized out of context for the African setting. This prompted further my desire to research on childhood in Uganda drawing on the Western informed theoretical training I had acquired.

I first conducted research in northern Uganda in 2008 as a master's degree student at Makerere University. As a student of gender studies, I was eager to understand the experiences of women in the conflict zones. I was, however, struck with the complexity in my conceptualization of a woman in relation to that of the local community. For instance, the individuals whom I had assumed to be children, given their numeric age were locally considered women due to the roles they performed. This triggered me to examine further what a child would be then. However, because it was not in the scope of the Master's research, I could not examine the issue as deeply as I desired. I only had the opportunity to continue this research as my Ph.D. area of focus. The theoretical grounding I received during my doctoral training, helped to situate and contextualize childhood and youthhood in Uganda as intersectional stages of human growth and development, which could not be contained in single categorical constructions. They are rather transitional and dynamic stages, which vary according to circumstances. In situations of displacement, for instance, children's potential to live protected lives free from violence, torture, and other victimizing processes is eroded. Children may find themselves actively involved in violent experiences. Thus, in this study, I set out to examine the Ugandan local understanding of childhood in relation to dominant Western constructions, examine the contradictions that arise and how these are harmonized, but also how armed conflict has impacted the local views on childhood. I also wanted to understand how recovery assistance programming operates amongst these situations. Most importantly I sought the self-identified understanding of the child and youth and generally centered the views of young people on childhood and violence.

As I wrote this book, I could not afford to relegate my personal childhood experiences, yet I focused on children in northeastern Uganda who have experienced armed violence as a daily lived experience. I acknowledge my privileged position as an educated employed woman, who has lived most of her life in the peaceful central region of Uganda. I am thus positioned as an "outsider-within". As a Ugandan raised, educated up to master's level, residing and working in Uganda, I am an insider yet because I come from the central region, studied my Ph.D. abroad (US), it positions me as an outsider. These positions help me to understand childhood experiences from a dual perspective but also multiply viewpoints situated in both African and feminist epistemologies.

Acronyms

ACHPR	African Charter on Human and People's Rights
ACRWC	African Charter on the Rights and Welfare of the Child
ICCPR	International Convention on Civil and Political Rights
IDMC	Internal Displacement Monitoring Center
IDP	Internally Displaced Person
KALIP	Karamoja Livelihoods Program
LRA	Lord's Resistance Army
NRA	National Resistance Army
NUREP	Northern Uganda Rehabilitation Program
NUSAF	Northern Uganda Social Action Fund
NUTI	Northern Uganda Transition Initiative
PRDP	Peace Recovery Development Plan
UDHR	Universal Declaration for Human Rights
UNCRC	United Nations Convention Rights of the Child
UNHCR	United Nations High Commissioner for Refugees
UNICEF	United Nations International Children's Emergency Fund
UNLF	Uganda National Liberation Front
UNSCR	United Nations Security Council Resolution
UPC	Uganda People's Congress

CHAPTER 1

Introduction

The chapters presented in this volume provide a critical assessment of mainstream Western constructions relating to childhood and how these impact children and youth in the developing world. The arguments are informed by a wide methodological approach largely anchored in feminist and African indigenous epistemological approaches. Research methods used included interviews, discussions, and observation. The volume has eight chapters, which are thematically linked to inform each other. The chapters discuss a number of issues related to the use of numeric age in categorizing the northern Uganda population, the naturalization of stages of human growth, the evolution of childhood, how armed violence impacts such constructions and the contestations emanating from the Global South lived realities and experiences.

Chapter 2, *Overview: Childhood and Armed Violence* provide a general overview of discourses on childhood in the Global South. It explores the complexities of defining who a child is using the context of the Global South. It is, however, a crucial stage that determines one's roles and responsibilities, entitlement, and levels of participation as well as identity and belonging. The understanding of childhood is, however, not static since it is informed by circumstances and thus shifts with time and space.

Chapter 3, *The Construction of Childhood*, explores the construction of childhood as a concept. It describes the historical base of the concept examining how it has evolved to the present state. The chapter

© The Author(s) 2018
V. F. Namuggala, *Childhood, Youth Identity, and Violence in Formerly Displaced Communities in Uganda*, Critical Cultural Studies of Childhood, https://doi.org/10.1007/978-3-319-96628-1_1

also expounds on the features of childhood that have been adopted as universal, paying special attention to chronological numeric age. I discuss how such hegemonic universalist understandings impact regions in the world that cannot live up to the ascribed standards. Children in situations of armed violence provide a good start on understanding how essentialist constructions and frameworks can have limited applicability. In situations of conflict, for instance, both children and parents (if available) may not know their age or dates of birth, there are unaccompanied minors as well as child heads of households who instead of being protected, must protect those under their care. I also discuss childhood as a human right looking at global, regional and national approaches to achieving children's rights. I conclude that imposing dominant notions of childhood to children in situations of distress is a colonialist approach that puts such children in more compromising situations since they cannot attain even the attributes recommended including security, protection, and education. Such colonial or neocolonial representations contribute to creating problematic portrayals of the range of childhoods in the third world by decontextualizing realities in such areas. It is thus crucial that specific social contexts under which children live are considered for the best interest and development of the child. As other scholars have noted, alternative ways of conceptualizing age (besides numeric age) that reflect children's lived realities need to be considered, including functional and relational age (Morrow 2011).

In Chapter 4, *Local Perceptions of Childhood, Youthhood, and Adulthood*, I explore alternative understandings to numeric age categorization, drawing on functional and relational age as critical in northern Uganda. The chapter discusses the complexities incorporated in understanding childhood(s) relating to individualism and collectivity. The main argument is that childhood in war-torn regions such as northern Uganda demands context-specific analysis since it cannot be accommodated by formal and universal understandings of childhood. This chapter argues that there is no single understanding of childhood, but rather various childhoods grounded in sociocultural perspectives. The chapter further discusses the dynamism in constructions of childhood in Uganda by exploring the transformations within the local understanding of childhood created by war by comparing pre-conflict and post-conflict communal perceptions to children and childhood. This chapter also expounds on childhood as a gendered construct with differentiated gendered experiences, needs, roles, and responsibilities.

Chapter 5, *We Are What We Are Not*, foregrounds the intersectional nature of youthhood focusing on female youth. The chapter examines the local understanding of "a youth" and how this plays out in access to and use of humanitarian assistance. I discuss the cultural relevance of the concept of youth to formerly displaced communities in Uganda. I argue that single categorical analysis is limiting in understanding the experiences of female youth who simultaneously occupy multiple categories. Teenage mothers, for instance, cannot fully pass as adults if they are not married. They can neither fit in the children's category because they have biological children, yet the youth category is locally understood to refer to young men. Female youth in such cases belong *everywhere* yet they belong *nowhere*, hence missing out on assistance and relief services, which target specific categories. Local communities find concepts like "child mothers" as belittling and constraining female youth's full identity as "real" mothers. Such out of context deframing externally constructed identity markers function to exclude specific youth.

Chapter 6, *Girlhood, Violence and Humanitarian Assistance*, focuses on humanitarian assistance as a major component of survival during situations of distress. Despite its contribution in saving lives, assistance has its own controversies especially from the perspective of the beneficiaries, which this chapter discusses. I examine the nature of aid provided and how respondents conceptualize it, the gendered experiences involved and the sociocultural dynamics that inform the implementation of assistance. This chapter also examines the link between aid and young people's participation in violence. I analyze how limited involvement of youth in humanitarian programs, public as well as cultural institutions may result in their increased involvement in violence. Challenges facing both recipients and humanitarian providers are as well discussed.

While young people encounter numerous challenges as the previous chapters demonstrate, Chapter 7, *Young People's Agency and Resilience*, acknowledges the organization and pliability young people portray during conflict and in post-conflict reconstruction. I stretch beyond war to include absolute poverty and disease outbreaks. Children are not entirely victims and vulnerable but also resilient and creative. Chapter 8, *Conclusion and Recommendations* provides the conclusion, including recommendations for reconstruction. The chapter also highlights areas for further research in relation to childhood and armed violence.

Reference

Morrow, V. (2011). *Understanding children and childhood* (Background Briefing Series, No. 1). Lismore: Centre for Children and Young People, Southern Cross University.

CHAPTER 2

Overview: Childhood and Armed Violence

Defining children and childhood, especially from a Global South perspective is no easy task (Abebe and Ofosu-Kusi 2016). Childhood in the Global South has several layers that are unsettled and contested using the Western eye, which is the dominant framework in defining childhood (Morrow 2011). The way childhood is conceptualized, however, determines one's identity, sense of belonging, entitlement, roles, and responsibilities. In situations of armed conflict, childhood status also determines the level of protection one is accorded as well as access to and use of humanitarian assistance services provided in the region (UNICEF 2016). In this volume, I explore and analyze how circumstances shape and influence the conceptualization of childhood, how local perceptions relating to children have shifted over the years due to armed conflict and displacement, and how children position themselves both during and after encampment and displacement. As such this volume defines a child as anyone who identifies as one or whom the community identifies as a child.

Armed violence impacts constructions and understandings of childhood at the global, regional, and local levels. This is due to breakdowns of socialization frameworks and processes. Drawing on experiences in northern Uganda, in this volume, I expound on causes, strategies, and impacts of war, especially on young people directly involved in and/or affected by the civil war. The volume further provides an analysis of humanitarian assistance programs implemented in the region and how this relates to the understandings of childhood. While societal contexts vary greatly and thus the understandings of childhood, formal and dominant childhood constructions are largely informed by the Western mainstream understandings of childhood. Such understandings often do not accommodate the local indigenous approaches especially in the Global South but also in poor regions in the Global North (Human Rights Watch 2005). This volume, therefore, discusses the specific attributes of childhood in Western and non-Western settings while highlighting the contradictions that emerge using the case of war-affected northern Uganda. Applying a Western perspective of population categorization has hindered access to and use of humanitarian aid among returned formerly displaced communities in Uganda.

In addition, I argue, with other scholars, that there is no single, universalized understanding of children, childhood, youthhood and adulthood, but rather various versions grounded in sociocultural viewpoints (Liebel 2012). While there are minor overlaps, for a more coherent flow, these two perspectives (the indigenous/local and the universal/dominant) are in this volume presented as distinct frameworks that largely contradict each other. I argue that externally framed perspectives distort and thus misrepresent the lived realities of communities in northern Uganda. Individuals in post-conflict northern Uganda live multidimensional lives that cannot be compartmentalized in restrictive, formal understandings of children, youth, and adults, largely grounded on numeric age. Evidence from findings suggests that these categories of growth and development are interrelated, connected, and at times overlapping. As such individuals cannot be entirely confined to singular categorical linear numeric age descriptions as the dominant narrative suggests. Besides chronological numeric age, population categories are also informed by functional and relational age (Morrow 2011). In northern Uganda, these alternative age descriptions determine roles, responsibilities, and entitlements and thus deserve consideration in explaining lived experiences of returned formerly displaced communities.

Using feminist and indigenous approaches, this book provides a critical analysis of cultural perspectives that exacerbate abuse and exploitation of children and youth in accessing humanitarian assistance. In addition, I consider other important identity markers that intersect with age including motherhood, wifehood, and (dis)ability among others to examine the complexities of identity among young people in northern Uganda. Childhood in this volume is examined under a specific situation involving displacement. It is therefore prudent that we explore global debates on displacement as a way of situating childhood in such circumstances.

CHILDHOOD AMIDST ARMED CONFLICT AND DISPLACEMENT

Childhood as a concept is contentious (Kendall 2008). UNICEF explains childhood as the "time for children to be in school and at play, to grow strong and confident with the love and encouragement of their family and an extended community of caring adults. It is a precious time in which children should live free from fear, safe from violence and protected from abuse and exploitation" (UNICEF 2005). With this understanding, childhood gets even more complicated in situations of armed violence given the breakdown in infrastructure, systems, and institutions (Cheney 2007). Children in situations of armed violence are effectively denied all requirements characterizing childhood. They may have no families, no protection, and no love, and are exploited physically, emotionally, and sexually, as the discussion to follow demonstrates. Humanitarian assistance provides some of these basic needs but due to differentiated understanding of a child between humanitarian agencies and the local communities, children's access and use of aid are hampered. In northern Uganda for instance, due to the protracted war, local perceptions and perspectives, expectations and roles relating to childhood changed to the disadvantage of children. What humanitarian agencies termed children using numeric age, were communally framed as adults in case they had biological children. This challenged programs specifically targeting children, which ended up benefiting the younger children to the disadvantage of the youth who self-identified or were communally identified as adults.

Children caught up in violent situations simultaneously experience victimization and active participation (Howard 2013). As vulnerable victims, children are exposed to enormous human rights violations including sexual harassment, death, and child soldiering and they form the majority of the displaced (Machel 2000; Soto 2009). Children, especially in African conflicts, have also actively engaged in violence including as combatants fighting for both government and rebel forces in several countries including Uganda, Liberia, Sierra Leone, Somalia and Sudan (Dolan 2009; Wessels 2006). In the northern Uganda civil war, child soldiering (boys and girls) has been a characterizing feature of the Lord's Resistance Army (Akello et al. 2006). The increasing involvement of children has been attributed to the changing nature of war reflected in the use of light weaponry. The issue of child soldiering has, however, received increased attention in the twentieth century and has become an international human rights issue, which governments and states are called upon to abandon (Howard 2013). Conflict scholars have argued that the use of underage soldiers has become a political issue largely informed by international actors including UNICEF, Human Rights Watch and Coalition to Stop the Use of Child Soldiers (ibid.). As such rehabilitation of former child combatants is a crucial component of the peacebuilding and reconstruction process of fragile states.

Perceptions of the use of child soldiers are context specific and have been changing globally even in the child protection instruments. When the United Nations Convention on the Rights of the Child (UNCRC) was established in 1989, the appropriate age for children to be included in fighting forces was 15 (ibid.). In the 1990s, this position was upgraded to a minimum age of 18 with the formation of the optional protocol to the UNCRC on the involvement of children in armed conflict. This protocol called for demobilization and reintegration of child soldiers. With all these instruments in place, child soldiering has persisted especially in sub-Saharan Africa and Uganda specifically. To clearly understand the situation in northern Uganda, it's crucial to have a broader approach to armed violence and internal displacement in the country. The following section provides an overview of Uganda's political state and persistence of civil wars.

Global Discourses on Internal Displacement

Displacement is a contemporary global challenge with brutal consequences for individuals, communities, structures, and systems (IDMC 2015). Armed conflict is also one of the leading causes of forced displacement and encampment. It results in local, regional, and global consequences, the most notable being internally displaced persons (IDPs[1]), refugees, violations of basic human rights, and inevitable demand for

---

[1] These are individuals or groups of people who have been forced or obliged to flee or to leave their homes or places of habitual residence, in particular as a result of or in order to avoid the effects of armed conflict, situations of generalized violence, violation of human rights or human-made disaster and who have not crossed an internationally recognized state border (UNICEF 2015: 14).

humanitarian assistance. By the end of 2015, out of the 41 million people who were internally displaced within their countries as a result of violence and conflict, 17 million were children (UNICEF 2016).

The Internal Displacement Monitoring Center (IDMC 2015) elaborates that intra-state conflicts can result in a "domino effect" on its neighbors. The Lord's Resistance Army (LRA) in northern Uganda provides a good example of this, given its active involvement in neighboring states including Central African Republic (CAR), the Democratic Republic of Congo (DRC) and South Sudan despite its Ugandan origin hence demanding integrated regional redress approaches. Forced displacement as a concept is wide and incorporates cross-border displacement and displacement from natural disasters.

This volume, however, focuses on internal displacement within Uganda's northern and northeastern region, which was largely caused by an armed civil conflict between the Lord's Resistance Army and the government of Uganda.

The meanings and causes of armed conflict are complex, divergent, and at times contradictory. These include religious fundamentalism (Puar 2007), poverty and unemployment (Urdal 2004), environmental degradation and corporate globalization (Shiva 2005), struggles for power and social inequalities (Dolan 2009) among others. Recent scholarship also points to high numbers of male youth in the population, commonly referred to as "youth bulge" as a security threat (Urdal 2004). Despite the ambiguity relating to its causes, what is common about war is that it affects children and youth in powerful and pervasive ways (Machel 2000; Spitzer and Twikirize 2013) hence the need to explore their views and experiences.

Feminist conflict scholars have critiqued the conventional understanding of war (Butler 2010; Sjoberg 2014). This is due to an oversight of gender, gender relations, and the gendered impact armed conflict presents. Conventional theoretical approaches to war have inadequately conceptualized what war is, who the actors are, the roles they play, and the gendered values in the making and fighting of wars (Sjoberg 2014). Feminist scholarship also challenges understanding and construction of war as an event that has distinct start and end dates and location (Sjoberg 2013). Feminist conflict scholars argue for instance that formal declarations of the end of violence and war do not necessarily result in peace for the local communities especially the women (Shepherd 2008), children and youth. In northern Uganda, it was clear that violence within communities and families had continued even after the 2008 official declaration of the end of the war and subsequent closure of IDPs camps. Another feminist critic is that armed conflict has been constructed in binaries of victims and perpetrators, which are understood to reflect women and men, respectively (Butler 2010). This disregards complex situations in which individuals simultaneously have multiple identities (Sjoberg 2014). Young people for instance were both victims and perpetrators of violence in northern Uganda. Thus, in this volume I adopt an intersectional approach to examining armed violence. The book includes an analysis of other identity markers with which gender operates, including age, motherhood, and marital status in situations of violence. I also acknowledge the multifaceted nature of identity, which children and youth in formerly displaced communities embrace.

By 2013, there were an estimated 33.3 million IDPs globally, which had by the end of 2014 increased to 38 million people (IDMC 2015). Sub-Saharan Africa and the Middle East are home to most of the displaced population. Specific countries such as Iraq, Syria, the DRC, and South Sudan present the highest percentages of IDPs. According to the IDMC, besides armed conflict, escalated numbers of IDPs have also been attributed to the changing nature of conflicts worldwide, including economic inequality as well as "protracted displacement"—a phenomenon explaining displacement that lasts more than five years (IDMC 2014). Populations affected by such protracted conflicts fail to link return, local integration, and peacebuilding. Ferris (2012) clarifies that protracted displacement is not static since IDPs move from place to place in search for security and livelihood sustainability. In Uganda, for instance, returned IDPs encounter protection and resource challenges in their return areas (Spitzer and Twikirize 2013). Returnees are involved in land disputes, marginalization, violence and consequently secondary displacement (Kindi 2010). The longer the conflict stays the more difficult it is to find sustainable solutions (Ferris 2012). Critical for this volume is that children and youth make a big percentage of the displaced and severely suffer its consequences.

Displacement at times can be explained by single factors including the struggle for power, disputes over natural and other economic resources and intercommunal violence. In many cases, however, displacement is an outcome of a complex mix of causes (IDMC 2015). The case of northern Uganda, for instance. has been attributed to unbalanced economic development, greed for political power (Dolan 2009) tribalism, as well as historical events (colonialism), and external intervention. This blurs simple explanations of the causes of violence and thus complicates conflict resolution. IDPs thus present a global challenge relating to humanitarian relief, and protection. Despite the multifaceted experiences IDPs undergo, they do not receive adequate support due to lack of systems and structures specifically targeting such population. IDPs remain under the care of their national governments which governments could be also responsible for their displacement.

The state of IDPs and their well-being are influenced by the guiding principles on internal displacement (2007). These principles are based on existing international humanitarian law and human rights instruments (OCHA 2003). They avail a substantive definition of IDPs as "persons or groups of persons who have been forced or obliged to flee or to leave their homes or places of habitual residence, in particular as a result of or in order to avoid the effects of armed conflict, situations of generalized violence, violations of human rights or natural or human-made disasters, and who have not crossed an internationally recognized State border" (OCHA 2003: 2). The guiding principles serve as an international standard to guide governments and humanitarian agencies on how to provide assistance and protect the IDPs. The guiding principles emphasize that persons who are internally displaced have the right to request and receive humanitarian assistance, while states and humanitarian actors have the responsibility to provide it (Fisher 2010). While these have been widely recognized, they are not legally binding and no institution is obliged to implement them. As such, nation states, NGOs, and humanitarian agencies are not held accountable for the situation of IDPs in their areas of jurisdiction. Scholars and activists have therefore noted that displacement is a clear representation of a war crime or a crime against humanity to which no one is held accountable (Branch 2007).

Brief Overview of Global Armed Violence

Armed conflict is one form of violence with serious consequences (Machel 2000). Besides claiming human lives, armed conflict hinders growth and development economically and politically, challenges enjoyment of human rights, and hinders access to social services like education and health. Violence, on the other hand, is a widely conceptualized phenomenon that affects virtually all facets of human life. It extends beyond the public to impact the private spaces—spaces that are traditionally understood to be peaceful (Sutton et al. 2008). Armed violence, therefore, brings together facets of armed conflict and violence.

Armed violence is simultaneously universal yet specific (Tripp et al. 2013). It affects both the developed and developing world although at different levels and in different forms. The nature of violence is dynamic and political conflicts instigated by ideological differences among superpowers are of less significance in the contemporary world (Rubenstein 1996). Wars, however, continue to rage in virtually every part of the globe, between and within nation states (Machel 2000; O'toole and Schiffman 2007). At the same time, war is specific in relation to individuals and communities whom it impacts in gender-specific ways through intersecting forms of class, age, gender, and nationality (Tripp et al. 2013). The degrees and levels of violence, however, vary depending on the social location of individuals within, between, and among groups (O'Toole and Schiffman 2007). Youth, for instance, are increasingly bearing the brunt of armed violence and atrocities (Spitzer and Twikirize 2013). In northern Uganda war, female youth specifically have been disproportionately affected.

Regionally, Africa's sub-Saharan region has been largely involved in armed violence especially in the twentieth century (Machel 2000). Countries like Uganda, Liberia, Somalia, DRC, Rwanda, Sudan, Sierra Leone, and Angola have been involved in such violence. Conflict scholars have attributed Africa's unceasing armed violence to the growing young population commonly described as a "ticking bomb" always waiting for a chance to explode. Young people in the developing world have a poor education with high levels of unemployment and generally, have poor living standards. They do not have much to lose, a fact that facilitates their participation in armed and other forms of violence (Urdal 2011). From this conceptualization, youth have created a security threat for not only Africa but also globally. Scholars have theorized this to be the youth bulge theory (Mesquida and Weiner 1999; Urdal 2004).

Armed Conflict and Forced Internal Displacement in Africa

Armed violence is a reality for much of contemporary Africa. By the end of 2015, there were 12.4 million people displaced internally due to violence (UNICEF 2016). Further still, Africa has the largest number of migrants globally and nearly one in three African migrants is a child. This makes the issue of childhood and children in situations of violence a very pertinent concern to Africa's development agenda. African-based armed conflicts end but many of them restart within a period of 10 years (Bigombe et al. 2000). This is typical because the root causes of such conflicts are never fully addressed. Due to armed conflicts, sub-Saharan Africa sends a big number of refugees to other continents, yet at the same time hosts several IDPs. Internal displacement is thus a critical concern in sub-Saharan Africa. While the statistics vary, researchers agree that Africa holds a huge number of IDPs. The IDMC notes that sub-Saharan Africa is home to one-third of the world's IDPs. By 2013, 12.5 million persons were dislocated within their nation states (IDMC 2014). Other scholars have observed that Africa holds five times more IDPs compared to refugees. By 2010, Africa had 2 million refugees as compared to 11 million IDPs (Ferris 2012). IDPs thus form a large percentage of the civilian population majority being women and children (Machel 2000). With limited corresponding frameworks in the form of structures and institutions, fragile states are created, which in turn breed violence (IDMC 2015). Sub-Saharan Africa has experienced unceasing intra- and interstate conflicts that have resulted in the massive internal displacement of people. Internal displacement is thus both a cause and consequence of armed conflict.

The increasing number of IDPs is due to several factors including the changing nature of conflict, especially in the form of strategy. The most recent fighting strategy directly targets the civilian population (Dolan 2009). The Lord's Resistance Army in northern Uganda targeted the young population using abductions and forced recruitment, and other civilians through maiming and mass killing. Besides the changing strategies adopted by conflict groups, battlegrounds are no longer fixed to distant areas away from the local communities. Instead, wars are fought within communities. Howard (2013) observes that in the twentieth and twenty-first centuries the frontline and home front cannot be disintegrated. This is also true for northern Uganda and neighboring Sudan and the DRC where rebels attacked villages, loot property in the form of food and animals, setting homes and fields on fire.

One other important key feature of contemporary conflicts is the wide involvement of young people as part of the armed forces, hence the concept "child soldiers," either voluntarily or through abductions and forced recruitment (McDonnell and Akallo 2007; Spitzer and Twikirize 2013). In 2008, the International Coalition to Stop the Use of Child Soldiers revealed that out of the 19 countries worldwide where children have been recruited in armed forces (both non-state and state armies), eight are African countries, all of which are in sub-Saharan Africa, Uganda being one of them. Despite the wide involvement of the youth population, conflicts and post-conflict reconstruction programs have not responded positively to their needs and concerns. Evidence for instance shows neglect of gendered perspectives and concerns (Coulter 2009; Sommers 2007).

Uganda's Political Contention and the LRA Insurgency in Northern Uganda

Uganda has been involved in civil and interstate armed conflicts since gaining independence from British rule in 1962 (Mutiibwa 1992). Interstate conflicts include wars with the Democratic Republic of Congo, and involvement in Somalia, Rwanda, and Sudan. The civil wars include various rebel groups like the Allied Democratic Forces (ADF) and the M23. Uganda's post-independence history has been characterized by civil wars and internal violence (Kasozi 2013). In 1966, Milton Obote, the prime minister at independence (1962) overthrew the president and declared himself the president of Uganda, after dissolving the British-preserved Monarchy (Buganda kingdom). Idi Amin, the head of armed forces, later deposed him in 1971. In 1979, Amin was also overthrown in a coup d'etat by a joint force between the Uganda National Liberation Front (UNLF) and the Tanzanian Army, and Yusuf Lule served as president for two months, only to be replaced by Godfrey Binaisa who was toppled within a year. In 1980, Milton Obote following an election won by his party, Uganda People's Congress (UPC), took on the presidency for the second time. This victory, however, was contested and Yoweri Museveni declared a war. In 1985 Obote was overthrown and replaced by Tito Okello. The following year, the National Resistance Army (NRA) overthrew Okello under the leadership of Yoweri Museveni, who has stayed in power to date (Mutiibwa 1992). A critical issue to address in this volume was the extensive use of children in the forces of the NRA.

The Ugandan civil war that has received much international recognition is the most recent and persistent one staged by the Lord's Resistance Army (LRA) in the northern part of Uganda. The LRA evolved out of the Holy Spirit Movement (HSM)—a rebellion started by Alice Lakwena in the 1980s as a divine mission to liberate the people of northern Uganda from oppression by southern tribes under the leadership of Yoweri Museveni. Joseph Kony took over leadership when Lakwena was exiled. He renamed the rebellion the Lord's Resistance Army, which has remained to the time of this writing. This civil war lasted over two decades and is described as the most overwhelming and persistent of Uganda's civil wars (Latigo 2008) as well as in recent African history (Spitzer and Twikirize 2013).

During this long conflict, both the LRA and the government of Uganda participated in crimes against humanity and violations of human rights (Branch 2007; Dolan 2009) including deployment of child soldiers, death of people, and displacement of others (Omach 2002; Soto 2009) resulting in the need for humanitarian aid and assistance (Gelsdorf et al. 2012). In examining the torture that communities suffered during the LRA conflict, Dolan (2009) compared what happened to communities in the war zones, especially in the protected villages, to that which happens in torture chambers. Dolan (2009) compared what happened to communities in the war zones, especially in the protected villages, to that which happens in torture chambers. Jan Egeland[2] visited the region and noted that little international attention had been accorded to fund the work for the children and their reintegration thus constituting a crisis describing the humanitarian situation in the region as "the worst humanitarian situation in the world" worse off than what was happening in Iraq (Dolan 2009: 23). The LRA armed violence is, therefore, a climax to these forms of violence (Moser and Clark 2001; Cheney 2007; Sjoberg 2014).

While the conflict started in the 1980s, the LRA atrocities intensified in the 2000s after the rebel group shifted its center to Southern Sudan (Soto 2009). Exiting Uganda halted attacks on the LRA from the Uganda government, which provided time for the rebels to restrategize and organize for more intensive attacks. South Sudan was the ideal place

---

[2]Jan Egeland, headed the UN Office for the Coordination of Humanitarian Affairs (OCHA). He made the comment during one of his visists in northern uganda in 2003. http://www.un.org/events/tenstories/06/story.asp?storyID=1300.

for this reorganization because it borders northern Uganda; yet, it was engaging in internal struggles and thus could not dedicate resources to fighting against a Ugandan rebel group (Branch 2007). This new location facilitated abductions, mutilations and confinement of abductees from Northern Uganda (Soto 2009). When they were relocated to new areas, communication and transportation back to Uganda was largely cut off. Chances of escaping were also minimal since abductees were in a foreign land. Adam Branch in his article, *Uganda's Civil War and the Politics of ICC Intervention*, argues that LRA atrocities also intensified due to arrest warrants issued by the ICC following the government of Uganda filing a case (Branch 2007). External involvement, in this case, worsened the situation for the local population.

In order to minimize LRA's atrocities to the civilian population, the Ugandan government forced the local populace into government-established protected villages (Dolan 2009). Government's conceptualization of protected villages is, however, different from the communal perspective as well as some critical conflict scholars. Branch, for instance, argues that protected villages are "most accurately identified as internment or concentration camps given their origin in forced displacement and continued government violence used to keep civilians from leaving" (2007: 181). In the camps, the population tortured on a mass scale by government and at times humanitarian agencies were also tortured, which scholars termed "social torture" (Dolan 2009). In this torture, over 80% of the local population was concentrated in "rural prisons", with extremely poor living conditions including restricted freedom of movement and association (Tim and Vlassenroot 2010: 14). The Ugandan government is thus accountable for imposing structural violence and systematic subordination to the people of northern Uganda (Dolan 2009). Both national and international humanitarian agencies are also liable for being complicit in this social torture since humanitarian workers operated through the structures of dominance instituted by the government and participated in human rights violations including sexual violence (Branch 2007; Dolan 2009).

In 2008, the president of Uganda, Yoweri Museveni declared northern Uganda a post-conflict region and while the formal declaration stands, it has not necessarily been followed by peace. Communities and youth specifically have continued to suffer in the postwar phase. This echoes feminist conflict scholars' observation that violence does not end in the war zone (Beijing 1995; Butler 2010) and peace is not just the absence of war (Shepherd 2008). War is rather carried back to the private spheres including families (Machel 2000; Shepherd 2008). As such, war is not an event that ends in the battlefield but a system, which infiltrates various aspects of survival (Sjoberg 2013). For women, there is nothing "post" about what is formally referred to as "post-conflict" since violence continues in the private spaces (Afshar 2003). It is this that young women in post-conflict northern Uganda face through sexual violence in the form of forced and/or early marriages, rape defilement and early pregnancies among others. To understand the complexity of war, Gregg Barack recommends a "change in the way we think about violence, non-violence and the relationship between the two" (2003: 4). This volume contributes to this while making specific reference to youth in northern Uganda. To understand what (non)violence is, I gathered young peoples' views and perspectives.

With the closure of camps, the government established decongestion sites (small settlements protected by the Uganda national army) where people were encouraged to relocate before eventually moving back to their original lands. Decongestion sites provided an in-between zone (borderland) that connected the IDP camps to the return areas and aided the transition. These sites were intended to fulfill the principle of voluntary return. A number of programs, including government programs like Northern Uganda Rehabilitation Program (NUREP) and Peace Recovery Development Plan (PRDP), were put in place to facilitate the return of formerly displaced persons into their communities. Such programs, however, did not specifically address youth voices, needs, and concerns. This volume observes that limited involvement and participation of young people is a major shortfall among reconstruction programs in northern Uganda and may consequently jeopardize the post-conflict reconstruction and peacebuilding process. A number of children and youth especially those that were unaccompanied have remained in the camp areas despite their official closure. Such a population has not yet received adequate attention and they are living in a more daring situation compared to those who returned to the villages.

Upon return from the battlefield (whether combatants or abductees), participants noted that generally former male fighters create a scare for the community. The local populations perceive them as violent. Their female counterparts, however, suffer stigmatization for crossing the line in relation to expected femininity. They are thus more vulnerable despite having experienced similar conditions (or even worse) with males.

One respondent in reference to female soldiers said for instance, "*do you consider those women? Who would let their son marry such? They are men dressed like women. Their hearts are not motherly. Which mothers kill? Women should support life and don't end it*".

The community assumed that whoever was abducted, definitely took part in ending life. Some girls, however, explained that they never held a gun in the bush. They instead served as wives, cooks and performed other domestic roles. Such negatively perceived identities hinder reintegration of youth on gendered grounds. Such girls are rejected from the category women/mothers due to roles they are suspected to have performed while in abduction. They are, however, at the same time also dismissed from the soldier category since it is largely understood to constitute men. Despite having similar or at times worse experiences compared to men, women do not receive the credit or compensation they deserve. With a clear picture of the northern Uganda conflict, I now delve into the impact externally imposed frameworks have on the formerly displaced population, especially, during the reconstruction phase. I pay special attention to children and youth.

The Impact of Dominant Western Frameworks on Global South Childhoods

Understanding Western frameworks relating to childhood and youthhood is crucial due to the fact that they inform the reconstruction processes and programs being implemented in northern Uganda. This book argues that post-conflict programs' minimal attention to children and youth specific concerns is a result of operating through dominant Western-based conceptualizations and theorizing relating to gender, childhood, and violence. Mainstream Western-based theories either do not represent or misrepresent the lived experiences of local communities, in this case, youth and children, in the Global South.

It is crucial that we conceptualize childhood from a cross-cultural perspective to avoid homogenization of experiences. Everyday realities of children are varied, they deserve specific approaches that reflect these complex situations. Acknowledging diversity, in turn, minimizes ethnocentrism and "othering" and demonizing of alternative notions of childhoods and children. We should, therefore, be looking at childhoods and not childhood given the variety of understandings and constructions depending on situations and location. The difference in understanding childhood ideas should not be treated as inferiority but rather as divergences created by circumstances and environments informing the local life experiences influenced by culture, class, and location among other things.

Feminism and Armed Violence

Feminists, however, realize that people at the margins for instance "individuals outside the halls of elite power are important to politics generally and war decision-making specifically" (Sjoberg 2013: 164). This justifies the need to study female youth in northern Uganda who are multiply marginalized socially, economically and politically yet at the same time they are actively involved in war situations. Gendering youth involvement in the war is thus crucial while avoiding shortfalls including the interchangeable use of gender and women and girls (Pratt 2011; Puechguirbal 2010, 2012). In studies where gender is applied, it is emphasized as a binary construction, which exacerbates victimization of women while reaffirming the masculine protective role (Bunch and Fried 1996). In other cases, the role of (adult) women is evoked at the expense of young women. The United Nations Security Council Resolution (UNSCR, 1325) for instance calls for participation of women in peacebuilding initiatives. Due to a focus on only gender, however, young women have been largely marginalized yet according to literature they suffer more oppression due to simultaneous occupancy of the "wrong" gender and age (Ang 2005; Boyden and de Berry 2004; Coulter 2009).

Intersectionality is imperative to transgress the stereotypical assumptions that women are either war victims or their agents but cannot be both. The failure to understand for instance the lived experiences of individuals especially youth as intersectional beings only partially captures what war is. The essentialist portrayals of women and children as inherently vulnerable and thus victims is a misrepresentation of those who participate as active combatants during situations of armed conflict for instance. Butler (2010) for instance demonstrates that "women make up a third of the militaries in Eritrea, Israel and Nepal, and women represent 11 percent of the US deployed troops to Iraq and Afghanistan, and 3 percent of the battle deaths" (40) yet literature continues to silence women's presence as fighters. Understanding the intersectional nature of violence brings out new questions and thus knowledge from previously suffocated voices. Examining such gendered intersectional avenues integrated into war helps demonstrate that while war is meant to be a public display of power, it ends up affecting the domestic aspects of the community in important ways.

One of the participants even described war to mean intra-personal trouble describing war as "that general lack of peace within a person". This means individuals can be at war with themselves and when this happens it can result in suicide due to the failure to find a reason for survival. This according to this participant is the worst form of war because it causes self-hate. Someone with such hate can do anything. Youth are always at war with themselves, which war is rooted in multidimensional aspects in the youth's life. Youth are at complex stages of their development biologically-struggling to decide who they are (adults, children) who to identify with; for instance, if one is a child mother, she struggles to identify with either of the groups. Youth social positioning is thus blurred and due to this, youth end up lost in the transition to adulthood. They become problematic to the elders, unruly yet still dependent. It is thus crucial to embrace intersectional approaches to war. These challenge conventional single categorical analyses largely grounded on only gender or even sex (Baden and Goetz 1997) or even age.

However, irrespective of their gender, age and other salient social identity markers, youth may simultaneously play the role of activists and parents, perpetuators, and victims (Moser and Clark 2001). Theories thus that emphasize youth's violent position miss out the complex picture especially during armed conflict. Intersectionality also enables analysis of intra-group power relations and deconstructing homogenizing tendencies in categorizing communities. In northern Uganda, I realized a gap towards the specific interests and concerns of young women who have been lumped up together as women simply because they are mothers. I believe that recognizing and addressing diversity within gendered categories as well as other intra-group differences is vital for establishing more sustainable gender equal societies. Female youth occupy a position distinct from that of adult women, which needs to be appreciated and critically examined.

Feminist scholars shift the boundaries beyond the binary constructions of gender that dominate the conventional analyses of violence to include socially non-conforming individuals (Shepherd 2008). In northern Uganda bodies that defy heteronormative social orders for examples youth that chose to stay single or delayed marriage and women who could not or did not what to have children encountered discrimination especially in the post-conflict phase. This, at times, led to limited access to resources like land given the patriarchal nature of the society where women access resources through male relatives especially husbands.

Indigenous scholars call for community security as a way of challenging Western conventional mainstream individualistic approaches that fail to capture violent experiences of most societies. From a feminist perspective, however, it is crucial to specify who is implicated in the "community". This necessitates accounting for cultural norms, group identities, structural violence and how these are connected to gender (Sutton et al. 2008). In northern Uganda it was clear that the female youth were largely neglected in the community. Their views, needs, and concerns did not receive the attention they deserved. This culminated in limited access to aid and use of aid meant for reconstruction of formerly displaced communities. Asserting the interests of the community as a whole, at times, undermines and/or naturalizes gender-age based inequalities. For instance, in some cases, girls that conceived out of rape were encouraged to marry their rapists as a way of encouraging communal solidarity. This greatly violates the rights of the girls and encourages male control over women's bodies and sexuality. Also, girls that were abducted and came back with children who are locally termed "rebel children" were stigmatized and discriminated as a way of maintaining unity. It is thus important to build normative conceptions of war that go beyond security as the absence of direct military threat (Shiva cited in Sutton et al. 2008) to acknowledge emotional battles within communities. This demonstrates how peaceful times are war times for particular community members.

In relation to the community, feminism further complicates the conceptualization of "woman" in understanding war. The concept woman has all through feminist theorizing proven problematic (Afshar 2003) and this discussion continues even in situations of conflict and violence. In analyzing policy, for instance, it is critical to specify which women, at what time and in what gendered way are identified and targeted. The local understanding of a woman also needs to be acknowledged. In northern Uganda, anyone with a child was considered a woman irrespective of her numeric age. While researching women, it is necessary to focus on experiences of women at the margins in traditional accounts of war making. Northern Uganda equates womanhood to motherhood and wifehood. This disregards age and other identity markers in this category, as well as inabilities to attain such set standardized notions consequently impacting power relations within the category, as well as access to available resources.

Given that violence manifests in complex networks, feminists call for a "gendered approach to human security focused on the linkages between the various forms of insecurity" (Tripp et al. 2013: 15). This challenges dichotomous constructions and emphasizes realization of connections between the private and public, individual and collective, and local and international dimensions to human life. Domestic violence for instance increases in situations of armed conflict (Moser and Clark 2001), and violence against women and girls often continues after wars have officially ended (Namuggala 2017) thus undermining the formalized distinction between war and peace that conventional theorizing accentuates. Peace therefore for women would mean, not just the absence of war but also the elimination of inequality and all possible sources of fear and threat including environmental concerns (Shiva 2005). For northern Uganda, such peace would mean increased access to resources like land, healthcare, and education, as well as protection from rape, defilement, and other forms of sexual harassment.

References

Abebe, T., & Ofusu-Kusi, Y. (2016). Beyond pluralizing African childhoods: Introduction. *Childhood, 23*(3), 303–316.

Afshar, H. (2003). Women and wars: Some trajectories towards a feminist peace. *Development in Practice, 13*(2), 177–188.

Akello, G., Richters, A., & Reis, R. (2006). Reintegration of former child soldiers in northern Uganda: Coming to terms with children's agency and accountability. *Intervention, 4*(3), 229–243.

Ang, F. (2005). *Children in armed conflict.* Boston: Nijhoff.

Baden, S., & Goetz, A. M. (1997). Who needs sex when you can have gender? Conflicting discourses on gender at Beijing. *Feminist Review.* No. 56, Debating Discourses, Practicing Feminisms (Summer, 1997), 3–25.

Barak, G. (2003). *Violence and nonviolence: Pathways to understanding.* London: Sage.

Beijing. (1995). *Fourth world conference on women, Beijing declaration.* http://www.un.org/womenwatch/daw/beijing/platform/declar.htm.

Bigombe, B., Collier, P., & Sambanis, N. (2000). Policies for building post-conflict peace. *Journal of African Economics, 9*(3), 323–348.

Boyden, J., & de Berry, J. (2004). *Children and youth on the front line: Ethnography, armed conflict and displacement.* New York: Berghahn Books.

Boyden, J., & de Berry, J. (2005). *Children and youth on the frontline: Ethnography, armed conflict and displacement.* London: Berghahn Books.

Branch, A. (2007). Uganda's civil war and the politics of ICC intervention. *Ethics & International Affairs, 21*(2), 179–198.

Bunch, C., & Fried, S. (1996). Beijing 95: Moving women's human rights from margin to center. *Signs, 22*(1), 200–204.

Butler, J. (2010). *Frames of war: When is life grievable?* London and New York: Verso.

Cheney, K. (2007). *Pillars of the nation: Child citizens and Ugandan national development.* Chicago and London: The University of Chicago Press.

Coulter, C. (2009). *Bush wives and girl soldiers.* New York: Cornell University Press.

Dolan, C. (2009). *Social torture: The case of northern Uganda, 1986–2006.* New York and Oxford: Berghahn Books.

Ferris, E. (2012). *Internal displacement in Africa: An overview of trends and opportunities.* Presentation at the Ethiopian community development council. Annual conference "Africa refugee and immigrant lives: Conflict, consequences, and contributions." https://www.brookings.edu/wp-content/uploads/2016/06/0503_displacement_africa_ferris.pdf.

Fisher, D. (2010). The right to humanitarian assistance. *Studies in Transnational Legal Policy, 47*, 41–128. http://heinonline.org/HOL/Page?handle=hein.journals/stdtlp41&div=9&g_sent=1&collection=journals.

Gelsdorf, K., Maxwell, D., & Mazurana, D. (2002). *Livelihoods, basic services and social protection in northern Uganda and Karamoja.* London: Feinstein International Center.

Gelsdorf, K., Maxwell, D., & Mazurana, D. (2012). *Livelihoods, basic services and social protection in northern Uganda and Karamoja.* Researching livelihoods and services affected by conflict (Working Paper 4). Feinstein International Center.

Howard, S. (ed.) (2013). Childhood in Africa. *An Interdisciplinary Journal, 3*(1). 2009 ISSN 1948-6502.

Human Rights Watch. (2005). Uprooted and forgotten: Impunity and human rights abuses in northern Uganda, Human Rights Organization. September 2005, vol. 17, no. 12 (A).

IDMC. (2015). *Global overview: People internally displaced by conflict and violence.* Geneva: Norwegian Refugee Council.

Internal Displacement Monitoring Center. (2014). *New displacement in Uganda continues alongside long-term recovery needs.* Retrieved September 30, 2015, from http://www.internal-displacement.org/sub-saharan-africa/uganda/2014/new-displacement-in-uganda-continues-alongside-long-term-recovery-needs.

Internal Displacement Monitoring Center. (2015). *Global overview, 2015: People internally displaced by conflict and violence.* http://www.internal-displacement.org/assets/library/Media/201505-Global-Overview-2015/20150506-global-overview-2015-en.pdf.

Kasozi, A. B. K. (2013). *The bitter bread of exile: The financial problems of sir Edward Mutesa 11 during his final exile 1966–1969*. Kampala: Progressive Publishing House.

Kendall, N. (2008). 'Vulnerability' in AIDS-affected states: Rethinking child rights, educational institutions, and development paradigms. *International Journal of Educational Development, 28*, 365–383.

Kindi, F. I. (2010). *Challenges and opportunities for women's land rights in post-conflict northern Uganda*. MICROCON Research (Working Paper 26).

Latigo, J. (2008). *Northern Uganda: Tradition-based practices in the Acholi region. Traditional justice and reconciliation after violent conflict: Learning from African experiences*. Stockholm: International Institute for Democracy and Electoral Assistance.

Liebel, M. (2012). Children's rights from below: Cross-cultural perspectives. *Studies in Childhood and Youth*. UK: Palgrave Macmillan.

Machel, G. (2000). *The impact of armed conflict on children. A critical review of progress made and obstacles encountered in increasing protection for war affected children*. The International Conference on War Affected Children. September 2000 Winnipeg, Canada.

McDonnell, F., & Akallo, G. (2007). *Why it matters and what you can do: Girl soldiers: A story of hope for northern Uganda's children*. Grand Rapids, MI: Chosen Books.

Mesquida, C., & Weiner, N. (1999). Male age composition and conflict severity. *Political and Life Science, 18*(2), 181–189. Beech Tree Publishing.

Morrow, V. (2011). *Understanding children and childhood* (Background Briefing Series, No. 1). Lismore: Centre for Children and Young People, Southern Cross University.

Moser, C., & Clark, F. (2001). *Victims, perpetuators or actors? Gender, armed conflict and political violence*. New York: Zed books.

Mutiibwa, P. (1992). *Uganda since independence: A story of unfulfilled hopes*. Trenton: Africa World Press.

Namuggala, V. F. (2017). *Gambling, dancing, sex work: Notions of youth employment in Uganda*. Brighton: Institute of Development Studies Press, University of Sussex.

OCHA. (2003). *Guiding principles on internal D=displacement*. United Nations Office for the Coordination of Humanitarian Affairs. OCHA Online Publication. http://www.ifrc.org/Docs/idrl/I266EN.pdf.

Omach, P. (2002). *Civil war and internal displacement in northern Uganda: 1986–1998*. Kampala: NURRU Publications.

O'toole, L., & Schiffman, J. (Eds.) (2007). *Gender violence: Interdisciplinary perspectives* (2nd ed.). New York and London: New York University Press.

Pratt, N., et al. (2011). Critically examining UNSCR 1325 on women, peace and security. *International Peacekeeping, 13*(4), 489–503.

Puar, J. K. (2007). *Terrorist assemblages*. Chapel Hill, NC: Duke Press.
Puechguirbal, N. (2010). Discourses on gender, patriarchy and resolution 1325: A textual analysis of UN documents. Special issue, women, peace and conflict: A decade after resolution 1325. *International Peace Keeping, 17*(2), 172–187.
Puechguirbal, N. (2012). The cost of ignoring gender in conflict and post-conflict situations: A feminist perspective (February 14, 2012). *Amsterdam Law Forum, 4*(1): 4–19.
Rubenstein, R. (1996). *Conflict resolution and power politics: Global conflict after the cold war*. Institute of Conflict Analyses and Resolution (Working Paper 10). George Mason University.
Shepherd, L. (2008). *Gender, violence and security: Discourse as practice*. London: Zed Books.
Shiva, V. (2005). *Earth democracy: Justice, sustainability, and peace*. Cambridge: South End Press.
Sjoberg, L. (2013). *Gendering global conflict: Toward a feminist theory of war*. New York: Columbia University Press.
Sjoberg, L. (2014). *Gender, war and conflict*. Cambridge: Polity Press.
Sommers, M. (2007). Embracing the margins: Working with youth amid war & insecurity. In L. Brainard & D. Chollet (Eds.), *Too poor for peace? Global poverty, conflict, and security in the 21st century*. Washington, DC: Brookings Institution.
Soto, R. (2009). *Tall grass: Stories of suffering and peace in northern Uganda*. East Lansing: Michigan State University Press.
Spitzer, H., & Twikirize, J. (2013). War affected children in northern Uganda: No easy path to normality. *International Social Work, 56*, 67–79.
Sutton, B., Morgen, S., & Norvkov, J. (2008). *Security disarmed: Critical perspectives on gender, race and militarization*. New Brunswick: Rutgers University Press.
Tim, A., & Vlassenroot, K. (2010). *The lord's resistance army: Myth and reality*. London: Zed Books.
Tripp, A. M., Ferree, M. M., & Ewig, C. (2013). *Gender, violence, and human security: Critical feminist perspectives*. New York: New York University Press.
UNICEF. (2005). *Childhood under threat. The state of the world's children 2005*. https://www.unicef.org/sowc05/english/childhooddefined.html.
UNICEF. (2016). *Uprooted: The growing crisis for refugee and migrant children*. New York: Division of Data, Research and Policy, UNICEF.
Urdal, H. (2004). *The devil in the demographics: The effect of youth bulges on domestic armed conflict, (1950–2000)* (Social Development Papers, Conflict Prevention and Reconstruction, No. 14).
Urdal, H. (2011). *A clash of generations? Youth bulges and political violence*. United Nations expert group meeting on adolescents, youth and development population division, Department of Economic and Social Affairs, United Nations Secretariat, July 21–22.

Wessels, M. (2006). *Child soldiers: From violence to protection*. Cambridge and London: Harvard University Press.
Wibben, A. (2011). *Feminist security studies: A narrative approach*. London and New York: Routledge.

CHAPTER 3

The Construction of Childhood

Introduction

This chapter traces the historical constructions informing global and regional understandings of childhood. These include the United Nations declarations on children and the African regional frameworks on childhood. The chapter also examines the Uganda national conceptualization of childhood. I, in addition in this chapter, draw linkages between these international, regional, and national frameworks and armed conflict. Specifically, I discuss the use of numeric age as a determinant of childhood (and adulthood) particularly focusing on Africa. The argument I make in this chapter is that generalized dominant notions of childhood have been informed by mainstream Western notions. As such they do not necessarily reflect the experiences of other regions especially those in the Global South, but also minority groups in the West. The chapter acknowledges that universalistic standards are crucial for the establishment of frameworks that set standards under which childhood safety can be generally monitored. However, when it comes to implementation of programs, universal frameworks need to be domesticated and localized to reflect specific recipient needs and concerns.

Several researchers and scholars have highlighted the fact that Western frameworks and approaches have had limited applicability to the Global South (Harris-Short 2003; Pillay 2014). There is, however, little articulation of the factors leading to this scenario. The one feature that some scholars have highlighted is the limited reflection to and integration of local cultures in externally framed approaches. Reichert (2006) emphasizes that countries and cultures resist imposition of universal human rights approaches when they contradict indigenous points of view. This chapter furthers this discussion focusing on the understanding of childhood in relation to youthhood and adulthood elaborating why Western informed humanitarian assistance programs have not served the needs of communities in the war-torn northern region of Uganda. The chapter centers on local perceptions of childhood in relation to dominant notions, which are reflected in humanitarian assistance programs. Dominant notions frame childhood from a human rights perspective to determine entitlements, roles, responsibilities, and obligations for children, parents/guardians, and governments. Contemporary narratives to understanding childhood, however, emphasize that childhood is neither universal nor static but rather a product of culture, which varies across time and space (Kehily 2009). It is thus crucial to appreciate and integrate progress cultural childhood notions into the mainstream frameworks.

HISTORICAL OVERVIEW TO DOMINANT NOTIONS OF CHILDHOOD

Childhood is analyzed in various ways including historical and biological approaches. As earlier stated, this volume takes on the sociocultural approach to childhood because the social justice framework ensures that the human rights of all children are promoted at all times (Johnny 2006). The sociocultural approach also brings out indigenous and feminist paradigms, the two epistemologies in which this book is greatly anchored. At the same time, the sociocultural approach examines how historical events and processes inform contemporary policy formulation and implementation. These, in turn, impact social relations and childhood. The sociocultural approach also acknowledges childhood as a product of a culture that varies in space and time (Jenks 2009), thus having specific sociocultural meanings (Gier 2006).

To understand the contemporary views on children and childhood, it is necessary to first explore the past and trace how the concept has evolved to its current meaning and stand. Several theorists have examined childhood. Each historic period has a different version of childhood (Mead and Wolfensten 1954). The general concession, however, is that there is "no consensus over the issue of childhood" (Jenks 1996: 2).

Childhood has generally been conceptualized in two broad categories, i.e. natural state of childhood and the social/cultural state of childhood (Boakye-Boaten 2010). Aries (1962) challenged the naturalization of childhood noting that this stage of development was less significant before the seventeenth century and children were treated as invisible beings. Jenks (1996) in agreement, emphasizes that "childhood is a historical and cultural experience and its meaning, its interpretations, and its interests reside within such contexts" (61). Children are thus dependent beings situated in relation to others (Johnny 2006). While children are social beings, childhood scholars have also challenged the dependency of childhood on adulthood arguing that children can be studied independently from adults (Chenney 2007; Kendall 2008). This is because children are differently and independently and, at times, uniquely affected by events and thus necessary to acknowledge the differences particular individuals have. Children in Africa for instance, have continued to face marginalization embedded in poverty, ill health, war (child soldiering) thus ranking poorly on well-being.

In addition, Qvortrup advances a structural approach to childhood adding class as a critical feature in understanding childhood. He argues childhood is "simultaneously a period in which children function as human and social beings, yet at the same time also a category of social class" (Qvortrup in Boakye-Boaten 2010: 105). From an African perspective, Qvortrup's argument is really applicable since children were considered assets for the family to provide labor and social security. Wealthy men, for instance, considered children as part of their wealth (Boakye-Boaten 2010).

Roussea (2011) accentuates that childhood is an independent stage in human growth that deserved to be treated independently of other stages. Consequently, societies began to consider children as independent beings and established institutional separations that catered for children (Chenney 2007). The institutionalization of childhood, however, restricted children's participation and freedom (Aries 1962). Childhood was treated as a stage of innocence and had great values that needed to be appreciated and guarded (Hendrick 1997 in Johnny 2006). These arguments to a large extent inform the current understanding of childhood as having distinct characteristics and hence an independent field of study. This belief was further resurrected by the welfare activists in challenging marginalization and calling for protection of children for instance by problematizing child labor, following the involvement of children in factory production (Johnny 2006). Welfare reformists emphasize that children need to be protected from harmful exposures including harsh labor, sexual exploitation, and child soldiering and this can be done through education. As such, governments and states have enforced a homogenized childhood through schools. While children's protection is necessary, such policies have, reinforced children's vulnerability and dependency on adults, state institutions, and systems (Johnny 2006). The protection narrative, therefore, resulted in the institutionalization of children and childhood as a way of preparing for the future. This hinders children's participation in economic activities as well as in the political sphere. It is this that Chenney (2007) has referred to as "differed citizenship". In situations like armed conflict where such protection cannot be accorded, it exacerbated children's vulnerability and frustration and bounds their self-esteem. Due to poverty, malnutrition, and sexual harassment, children in war zones are "left more marginalized by knowing their universal rights" (Chenney 2007: 17) since such rights cannot be actualized in their daily lives.

In the twentieth century, the protection argument was adopted by political parties, and this greatly increased the value states attached to children (Cunningham 1995). According to the protection perspective, children are to be protected until the age of 18 when they attain adulthood. Several state governments drafted laws and policies geared toward children-specific services creating more coherence for the dominant (numeric age) construction of childhood. This entirely disregarded the alternative conceptualizations of childhood and adulthood, for instance, those reflected in functions one performs and the relations they have with others (Morrow 2011). Despite the limitations, dominant mainstream perspectives on childhood have continued to greatly inform the contemporary global perceptions of childhood (Stasiulis 2002). Emphasizing mainstream Western ideologies of innocence and contentment, however, discounts children in distress situations for instance war zones, where ideal childhood expectations are practically unrealizable. The United Nations Convention on the Rights of the Child (UNCRC) for instance largely focuses on protectionism (Johnny 2006). Children's active participation is still limited in many societies due to immaturity expected by society hence dependency on the state and adults to make decisions on behalf of and for the children. While it is not always the case, adults are expected to act in the best interest of the child hence restricted direct involvement of young people on issues, which absolutely concern them. However, responsible adults have severally neglected children-specific needs and concerns. In addition, promoting adult views on children's rights on behalf of children disempowers the children and frames them as entirely vulnerable (Smith 2002). Socialized victimization and vulnerability is exacerbated in fragile situations like armed conflict, where the implementation of protective mechanisms is highly challenged due to broken institutions and structures. As such, children's rights in situations of distress are violated and standardized childhood is thus inapplicable. Researchers have referred to such childhood as "stolen childhood" due to poor health, malnutrition, extreme violence, child marriages, and child labor among others (Save the Children 2017). Below is a more intrinsic discussion relating to the right to childhood.

The Right to Childhood

The universal declaration of human rights, article 1 states "all human beings are born free and equal in dignity and right". In this capacity, children's rights are human rights. Children's rights, therefore, impact how children are perceived as members of society (Wall 2008). The UNCRC defines children's rights as "a set of universal entitlements for every child and young person below the age of 18. These entitlements apply to every child of every background and encompasses what they need to survive and have opportunities to lead stable, rewarding lives" (Save the Children 2006: 4). The definition of children's rights is, however, a contentious issue and no single definition has been unanimously accepted by both academics and practitioners (Morrow 2013; Kendall 2008). Boakye-Boaten (2010) argues this disagreement is due to the political claims attached to childhood and the notions of identity claimed through the different cultures. As such, children's rights will only change society if the whole concept of human rights is reimagined in light of childhood (Wall 2008).

The main instrument for understanding human rights is the Universal Declaration for Human Rights (UDHR), which provides for basic human rights principles. Specific children's rights are, however, detailed in the UNCRC (1989). This is the standard global instrument for the protection of children. This instrument elaborates the United Nations' position on protection of children from, among other things, hazardous activities like child labor and recruiting them as soldiers. The convention encompasses survival, protection, participation as well as development rights relating to children (Andrews and Kaufman 1999). The UNCR convention elaborates that children just like other human beings are born with fundamental rights and freedoms but with particular additional special needs due to their vulnerability. While the convention is very elaborate and clear, scholars argue that understanding and application of human rights cannot be accomplished without a clear understanding of universalism and cultural relativism as critical concepts relating to childhood (Reichert 2006). As such in article 1, UNCRC defines child to be "a person below the age of 18 unless the laws of a particular country set the legal age for adulthood younger". This treaty, therefore, creates room for local specificity as a way of accommodating variances in understanding and conceptualization of adulthood. However, given the power relations at hand, most countries in the Global South, including Uganda have not taken on this condition but instead adopted and maintained the dominant understanding and set eighteen as the age of attaining adulthood. Such applications disregard the context relevant and locally specific characteristics defining childhood.

In academia universalism and cultural relativism have been framed as binary categories. For instance, Harris-Short (2003) highlights how academic discussions focus on Western tendencies of universalism while non-Western tendencies are used to emphasize cultural relativism. I, however, argue that understanding these (universal and cultural relativism) as binaries downplays the intersectional complexities that emerge in situations of for instance forced displacement where simultaneously both apply and inform the experiences of children.

In academia, Childhood Studies is a recent field that explores the experiences of children (Kehily 2009). This field of study, however, has been dominated by the mainstream Western understanding of childhood (Morrow 2013). This dominant construction has marginalized alternative forms and constructions of childhoods, especially those in the developing world but also minority groups in the developed world (Human Rights Watch 2007). Specific childhood experiences deviant from the normalized perspectives for instance in contexts including situations of armed violence have also not received the attention they deserve (Cheney 2007). While childhood as a specific field of study is new, the study of children and childhood(s) has been an integral part of other academic disciplines for a long time (Kehily 2009; Morrow 2011). Childhood has for instance been emphasized in sociology and cultural studies, while education and psychology have focused on the child/children. Interdisciplinary fields of study including international relations (Sjoberg 2013, 2014), women and gender studies, as well as research informed by feminist and indigenous epistemologies (Chilisa 2012; Wane 2013; Oyewumi 1998) have, on the other hand, drawn attention to more complex understandings by integrating these various aspects simultaneously. This book builds upon this complex interdisciplinary approach by incorporating armed violence and forced displacement as critical concepts in studying childhood in Africa.

Outside academia, interest in children's rights has also increased due to overwhelming violations of children's rights globally and generally escalating violation of human rights (Kendall 2008). The issues of concern among both scholars and practitioners are broad and diverse including child soldiers, child labor, education, health, media (pornography, advertisement, and film), child trafficking, child prostitution, and the right to play among others. I discuss many of these in this volume, exploring how they relate to and impact the understanding of childhood in war-torn northern Uganda. In addition, I explore how these concerns manifest differently between experiences in the Western and non-Western countries. I wish to clarify that while I use the categories "West" and "non-West", I am aware that these terms are essentialist (Mohanty 2003) and do not necessarily depict the lived realities of communities within these regions. No unitary construction of childhood exists in either Western or non-Western regions, and childhood constructions are informed by context and lived experiences (Morrow 2013). Kehily (2009) importantly elaborates that Western conceptualization of the child subsists to reaffirm power hierarchies between the West and the non-West. In situations of distress, such power relations are manifested through a number of approaches including humanitarian aid, conceptualization, and categorization of the population. With this in mind, I wish to clarify further that "Western" in this volume unless otherwise stated specifically refers to mainstream dominant constructions of childhood in the developed world.

Childhood has been evolving over time and is ideologically and socially constructed depending on given particular situations. The current understandings of childhood can thus be both socially and historically traced (Johnny 2006). This volume particularly centers on the social work perspective that prioritizes fairness and equal opportunities in accessing state resources to ensure children's care and protection

(Pillay 2014). This perspective follows a social justice framework. It acknowledges that since childhood is socially constructed, there are varying understandings, expectations, and entitlements accruing to children, which also vary with time. As a social construct, childhood demonstrates that society's expectations are tagged to race, class, gender, and location among other identity markers. All these influence children's enjoyment of human rights.

Review of relevant literature provides the historical construction of childhood in the Western world and how this understanding has over time become shaped as the standardized view informing global childhood standards (Howard 2013). Contemporary childhood narratives have been grounded from the human rights framework, framing children's rights as universal and indispensable (UNCRC 1989). Such universalistic approaches to childhood have, however, been critiqued for imposing Western imperialistic views on to other regions (Boakye-Boaten 2010), most important for this discussion being Africa. Universalism perpetuates colonialist practices against the "other", and human rights are used as the tools by the West to impose their views through political and economic dependence (Harris-Short 2003). The same critique also goes for children's rights for being imperialistic and imposing Western culture unto children in the Global South (Ignatieff 2001). This is because human rights downplay the importance of the local cultural and legal frameworks. The local population continues to encounter a standardized version of international human rights law that hardly adopts and responds to local cultural narratives. In reference to education, for instance, one respondent questioned the value of education in a context where one is not assured of a livelihood. She noted:

> Education is good? For who? The government? I will tell you many of our children don't go further to qualify for educated people's jobs. Now if they also don't train for the substance survival work, they end up in-between and half baked, unable to do both...The only thing we have control over is our children and we shall continue doing what we believe is right as parents.

Education is a human right and children should access education irrespective of the region of the world where they are raised. Education should, however, be meaningful and useful to its recipients. To achieve this, such education should be domesticated to provide socially relevant knowledge, but also practically applicable skills for sustainability of the local population. This emphasizes the fact that education should not entirely be formal in situations where societies have practical challenges. In his speech on education for self-reliance, the former president of Tanzania, Julius Nyerere explained that children can benefit from learning informed by living and doing. He emphasized that the purpose of education is "to prepare young people to live in and to serve the society, and to transmit the knowledge, skills, values, and attitudes of the society. Whenever education fails in any of these fields, then the society falters its progress, or there is social unrest as people find that their education has prepared them for a future which is not open to them" (Nyerere 1968: 269). This clarifies that education that doesn't strategically integrate the society separates its trainees from the societal realities which education is ideally meant to engage with hence rendered useless for those particular societies.

With the wide raging unemployment in Africa generally and Uganda specifically (Namuggala 2017), the participant in the preceding quote is socially suited to question whether education is helping the community or not. She emphasizes the importance of survival technics in a region where famine is rampant due to natural calamities but also agricultural production hampered by the protracted war in the area. Being on the borderline between education and illiteracy has affected identity formation and self-definition by the young people since they cannot fully identity with either category. This parent seems to conclude that "half baked"/half-educated youth are worse off than the uneducated ones who would fit the cultural expectation.

In addition, international human rights law promotes pathologization of alternative cultures and calls for distortion and extinction of such cultures in favor of the superior external culture (Harris-Short 2003). This creates a binary between the universal rights and the local perspectives to childhood in Africa. A critical example of a conflicting concern is on child labor. In the context of sub-Saharan Africa, child labor is a very tricky undertaking. In the sociocultural perspective, preventing poor children from working is often harmful to them since they work to acquire the basic needs including food and clothing (Bass 2004) education fees, stationery, and uniforms (Bourdillon 2006). The local communities in northern Uganda also share a similar perspective. Several respondents explained that children have no choice but to work because they must fulfill school requirements in addition to helping to sustain their families. The school going children are required to have school uniforms (for safety and smartness) and also buy scholastic materials including books and pens hence children work to supplement provisions made by parents and guardians. Children can therefore not afford to only learn but rather work and study concurrently.

Besides working for pay, in sub-Saharan Africa, laboring especially within the family and on community programs is a core component of the socialization process (Boakye-Boaten 2010) and thus a system of initiation into adulthood. In Uganda specifically, child labor has been constructed and socially understood as a family support venture that affirms a sense of unity and belonging. In an indigenous Ugandan paradigm, child labor, especially within families, is perceived as an ongoing process of vocational training and part of socialization relevant for community survival and individual adult sustenance. Failure of parents to train their children in culturally relevant skills is thus termed betrayal and sabotage in the children's transition to adulthood. According to one female clan committee member,

> Making your children not to work is the worst thing any parent can do to their children. That's promoting laziness! Who survives in the world without working? How? Tell me. We all have to work and our children should work right from a young age to develop such skills. The earlier you learn to work, the easier it gets in adulthood.

What is institutionally termed as child labor and thus needs to be prevented contradicts the local perceptions. Local communities consider children working as part of socialization, which does not constrain the child in any way but rather prepares them to fit in the community and survive well during adulthood. Universal discourses in such situations set apart children from their local societies instead of integrating them for sustainability. The "ideal child" according to international frameworks contradicts the local context in most African settings (Chenney 2007) not to mention children in war-torn regions. UNICEF (2005) for instance describes childhood as a time for children to be in school and at play, to grow strong and confident with love and encouragement from their families. Children are thus expected to live free from fear, safe from violence, abuse, and exploitation. The state and family are responsible for providing such protection for the children and this responsibility is legally binding. States that ratify the treaty are therefore held accountable for the rights of children within their jurisdiction (UNICEF 2005).

Such a description defines children as entirely dependent on the guardians, parents, and elders around them (Parter-Brick and Smith 2000). It revolves around fortification of children and focuses on vulnerability, victimhood, and innocence narratives. In cases like northern Uganda, the would-be protectors (state) has participated in the violation of the rights of children through encampment and forced displacement (Dolan 2009). State and guardian protection is embedded in innocence narratives, a perspective that positions children as essentially passive and helpless. Children are portrayed as lacking choice and control over what happens in their lives. However, in situations of violence and war, this understanding is debatable since children can be both victims and perpetrators of violence. Dichotomized descriptions of passive vs active are thus limited given the intersectional nature of position children in such situations occupy.

In northern Uganda, the moral and legal perspectives to human rights conflict the local realities, which permits resistance from the local communities. Promoting international declarations without consideration of local social realities, therefore, imposes the hegemonic view to childhood and consequently hinders its success. Emphasizing Western notions of childhood would, therefore, exacerbate the cycle of poverty and dependency in regions like northern Uganda, which rely entirely on agriculture and animal production. It is, therefore, necessary for human rights activities and humanitarian assistance programs being implemented in the region to harmonize their formal conceptualization with the local narratives. This would minimize resistance from the local population and also ensure sustainability for the benefit of the children targeted.

Besides cases of working to supplement their families' survival, children in northern Uganda are in some instances heads of households and thus the sole providers in such situations. As household heads, laboring for survival is inevitable (War Child 2015). Without a welfare system that can provide child protection centers, coupled with changed communal attitudes toward adoption of children, child labor avails a source of survival and livelihood for war-affected children. The need for survival has resulted in the involvement of children in socially, morally and legally compromising activities including prostitution, and human trafficking as a way of obtaining basic needs. Even though community discredits such activities, the lack of viable alternatives sustains them, especially, among the young people. Important contradictions therefore arise with international/Western child rights frameworks that challenge child labor.

As a way of challenging child labor, some humanitarian agencies have asserted that the right to play is ideal for children's proper development and upbringing. In the Western context, play is a regulated activity with specified time as well as particular toys marked for specific ages and genders (Parter-Brick and Smith 2004). The study participants, however, noted that play in the context of local northern Uganda does not have to have specific time allocated and can be performed during work time, especially given the heavy workload returning communities have. One married mother of 7 with two deceased bitterly noted,

> What is the importance of playing when you sleep hungry? Or maybe I should say can you play when you are hungry? All the bushes are over grown, we have no food and you talk about play? That's not our problem... I have not heard, all my life, of a child who died because of not playing. But I have witnessed children die of hunger. They (NGOs and government) say playing is about exercising but working is too! You just honestly cannot set time aside for play. Children play as they work for instance on their way to the well, they go playing with each other.

In the preceding case, it is evident that the conceptualization of play is different for both humanitarian agencies and local communities. The understanding of childhood that humanitarian programs advocate is contextually inapplicable. This has resulted in resistance from the local population. It is therefore crucial that a middle ground can be reached, a ground that accommodates the needs and concerns of the parents and guardians yet at the same time giving children an opportunity to play. Besides the limited cultural and social applicability, giving children playtime also has gendered implications. Like explained earlier, children in Uganda work with other family members to sustain the family and at times households. As such, women work with their children to accomplish domestic chores. Awarding children playtime therefore would mean freeing the children of their household roles. Since most household tasks are a social responsibility of the women, playtime affects the workload women partake. As such, girls who do most of the domestic chores would rarely be given playtime. Boy children would end up having relatively more free time, which is allocated to play compared to the girls.

To engage dominant notions that envisage play as a specific activity defined by gender and age among other factors, I recommend cultural relativism to provide contextual relevancy of play. Cultural relativism avails an alternative to universalism, which fronts dominant cultures as the standard upon which all other alternative cultures are measured. Unlike universal cultural frameworks, cultural relativism portrays all cultures as equal. As such foreign values should not be framed as superior to the local culture but rather work with them for the fulfillment of children's rights. This book acknowledges cultural differences as crucial for understanding children and childhood. At the same time, it also elaborates that local cultures are not homogenous but rather dynamic and influenced by situational factors including war and displacement. Situations like war affect traditions and practices in recognizable ways, thus facilitating their transformation as a way of everyday survival. The book thus critically assesses the local values by examining the social systems and structures that inform cultural beliefs and practices following post-conflict. This informs understanding of how human rights are applied to everyday experiences of local communities in war and post-war situations. This volume focuses on humanitarian assistance provided to formerly displaced communities in northern Uganda recognizing children and young people as agentic beings and thus prioritizing their views and voices.

As explained in the preceding discussion, universalistic frameworks have enormous limitation, especially, when applied to the African context. This book, however, also observes that universalistic frameworks have a positive role to play in society. Universalistic frameworks are crucial in guiding global childhood standards, a case in point being the 1989 UNCRC. Such generalizable standards measure levels of development, enjoyment of human rights and states' accountability to these standards. However, when such tools are not domesticated during implementation, it halts their applicability to local settings. Since cultural values and identity define who people are, then the failure to acknowledge cultural differences is itself a human rights violation (Reichert 2006). This is because "cultures are a unique whole with parts so intertwined that none of them can be understood or elevated without reference to the other and to the cultural whole" (Lawson 1998: 13). A detailed specific analysis of this in northern Uganda is provided in Chapter 2.

Protection of children is highly acknowledged and thus advocated by both practitioners and academics. Some Childhood Studies theorists, however, have argued differently calling out for active full participation of children (Boyden and Berry 2004). This is because the vulnerable and victim portrayal of children is not a true representation of the lived experiences of children in many parts of the world (Holt 1994) especially in

Africa and childishness is not a biological feature but rather situational. For instance, children who participate in farming or pastoral activities learn responsibility earlier in life (Chenney 2007) and hence give up childhood way early in life. Full participation of children problematizes the dominant perspective of childhood as determined by numeric age, which is emphasized by the dominant views. Active participation of children irrespective of their numeric age promotes the agency rights of children. Childhood should thus be conceptualized as a stage, which incorporates together biological and social processes (Scheper-Hughes and Sargent 1998). It, in addition, intersects individual and communal processes and thus should be understood as such to capture a holistic picture of childhood in Africa. Contemporary understandings have incorporated all these various aspects to define children's rights as "human rights of children with particular attention to survival, development, protection and participation" (Nikku 2012: 51). This book also largely anchors in this integrated conceptualization of children and childhood.

The major contemporary global debates on childhood within and outside academia are largely constructed in two perspectives—protection and participation (Liebel 2012). I find it important to elaborate on these perspectives since I use them in discussing the contradictions between mainstream Western and northern Uganda childhood constructions later in the book. Protection narratives largely disregard the perspectives of children. Western conceptualizations of childhood, which emphasize innocence and dependence, undermine children and youth active participation (Johnny 2006). This study finds it clear that there are important differences in perspectives of children and adults as well as within the broad category of children due to their gendered expectations and experiences. I thus agree with Leanne Johnny's conclusion that "the social construction of childhood within Western societies has resulted in the creation of an immature and dependent representation of young people" (ibid.: 17), which has been passed on to other regions of the world.

The protection and vulnerability theory is counteracted with the participation theories. These prioritize children's independence, agency and thus active involvement in all aspects especially those affecting their lives. In situations of armed violence, the child participation framework elaborates on children's ability to resist and adapt to changed situations at times better than the adults (Fernando and Ferrari 2013), make well-informed decisions (Offit 2008), and take on roles previously conceptualized as adult roles in the pre-conflict setting (Spitzer and Twikirize

2013). In situations of violence, the participation theory argues that children are not entirely victims but rather at times active participants. They may for instance voluntarily offer to join the armed forces and freely involve in crimes against humanity including murder and rape (Cheney 2007). They thus need to be accorded attention by listening to their concerns and needs to inform resettlement and reintegration within communities to avert future conflicts.

The dominant conceptions of childhood have been termed ethnocentric (Boyden 1997). The international frameworks portray the Western view of childhood as the "correct" childhood upon which other regions are judged irrespective of the various environmental circumstances. The dominant view is promoted and imposed through the media, aid agencies (Chenney 2007), which stigmatizes alternative notions of childhood.

Another critical feature of dominant childhood constructions is individualism. Global rights frameworks construct children as sovereign individuals yet in Africa, cultures dictate that the community takes precedence over the individual (Chenney 2007) although the individual is allowed to blossom within the community (Wane 2011). The preamble to UNCRC acknowledges that every child be fully prepared to live an individual life in society (Andrews and Kaufman 1999). At 18 when childhood ends, children are held individually responsible legally and economically for their actions.

Besides external hegemonic views, the long war had substantial impacts on the local notions of childhood. The displacement and encampment created idleness which greatly affected children and youth. They thus have a difficult time integrating suitably into the community because of the work-free childhood they had in the camp. Young people lack the skills required to thrive in the rural setting given their upbringing, which was not only urban-centered but also confined and restricted in movement and socialization with the older generation. Because youth lack the necessary survival skills, they resort to criminal and violent activities reproducing assumptions in theories like the youth bulge theory that define poor young men as violent. Dominant universal frameworks, therefore, recreate the negative connotations such frameworks have on the developing world and its people.

The previous discussion clarified on the transformations that have led to the current understanding of childhood. The following section examines how Africa as a region fits into the global childhood debate, the impact it has on African children and the factors explaining childhood narratives in Africa.

Childhood in Africa

Africa is varied, diverse, and complex, and this volume does not claim to homogenize childhood on the continent in any way. However, given the continent's historical legacies, some generalizations especially on the problems it's facing, and thus, hindrances to children's rights can be made (Boakye-Boaten 2010). The rights of children in Africa have changed and improved over time especially in terms of policies and frameworks geared toward the rights of children and young people generally (Howard 2013). As earlier on elaborated, the standard measure has been the mainstream Western construction of childhood. Over the years, the concept of childhood has been institutionalized through policies and treaties to which most African states are signatory including the African Charter on the Rights and Welfare of the Child (ACRWC). These formalized systems have altered and at times replaced the traditional socialization processes in Africa. For instance, the goal of "political institutions changed from protecting members of society to the maintenance of law and order" (Boakye-Boaten 2010: 111). For instance, children are forcibly pulled off the streets without clear indications of where to go, without handling the causal factors drawing them to the streets.

Generally, childhood in Africa has been framed as a site of intervention for the developed world. Media portrayals as well as research concentrated on the hegemonic negative representations of the continent reflected in hunger and starvation, armed violence (child soldiers) and displacement (internally displaced persons, refugees, and street children), HIV/AIDS, corruption and dependency on foreign aid and assistance, and high infant and maternal mortality rates (Abebe and Ofusu-Kusi 2016). Such representations are partial explanations of what happens in Africa. The portrayals are limited due to the fact that they are produced by adults with minimal involvement of children, if any. The majority of such researchers are often non-Africans who try to conceptualize African childhoods using their dominant foreign lens (ibid.). In addition, partial portrayals disregard agency and resilience among the African people. It is, for instance, important to acknowledge how children survive amidst such challenging situations like armed conflict and forced displacement.

Understanding childhood as a social construct is the most applicable approach to the African context (Boakye-Boaten 2010). In traditional Africa, the community in the form of clans, families, and villages have collective responsibility for the children (Swadener et al. 2000). This structure provides protection and guards against the abuse of children (Kilbride and Kilbride 1990). However, since the cultural organization is dynamic, the African cultural and social structures have evolved especially due to globalization in the form of international frameworks standardizing childhood, education, political, and legal involvement in the upbringing of children.

Despite the formally institutionalized policies, the implementation of children's rights is still lacking which has minimized realization of children's rights as defined by these frameworks. Limited implementation is explained by a number of factors as discussed below.

Lack of committed leadership to foster children's rights is a big hindrance to the realization of children's rights. Pillay (2014) argues that African leaders are just not taking children's rights seriously. For instance, some countries do not have representatives to the committee of experts, while others have severally failed to submit annual reports on the progress and advancement of children's rights in their respective countries. In the case of Uganda, cultural and other local leaders have not been efficiently involved in institutionalized childhood frameworks. As such, the local perceptions to childhood have not been represented and frameworks not localized to suit locally relevant opinions relating to childhood development.

Another generalizable feature throughout Africa is the lack of democracy to facilitate awareness of human rights (Sewpaul and Mathias 2013). Sub-Saharan Africa, for instance, has been marred by political instabilities especially war, armed conflict (civil and cross-border), and violent protests. Violence and conflict scholars have theorized high numbers of young people in the population as a security threat in what is referred to as "youth bulge theory". Children are both victims and perpetrators of violence for instance through child soldiering (Blattman and Annan 2009; Machel 2000). Africa's population has been continually growing young due to among other factors HIV/AIDS and war (Chenney 2007), resulting in increasing numbers of orphans and child-headed households. On average, 65% of Africa's population is less than 35 years old (*Africa Renew* May 2013). In Uganda specifically, despite legal frameworks and prohibitions, child soldiers have been a characteristic feature of the country's civil wars since the 1980s (Mutiibwa 1992; Sptizer and Twikirize 2013). This indicates how much important it is to involve youth and young people generally in creating peace and stability in Africa. Competing priorities like insecurity, war, and violence hinder Africa's concentration on the rights of children and these, end up ranked lower than security and other issues.

Government of Uganda's Perspective on Childhood

At the national level, the Ugandan construction of childhood relies largely on the child protection theories. International discourses, for instance, those promoted by UNICEF and CRC suit the Ugandan government's approach to child development (Chenney 2007). The 1995 constitution adopted the Western numeric age approach and defines a child as "a person below the age of eighteen years". Uganda in 1990 ratified the UNCRC, hence the obligation to implement the convention's tenets. In 1996, the government established the Children's Statute with the aim of improving survival, development, and protection of children (Evans 2001 in Cheney 2007). Other legal tools intended to protect children in Uganda include laws on marriage, child labor, and political participation. Despite the rhetoric about the rights of children, a big number of children in Uganda are powerless, marginalized, and at times exploited due to their situational daily experiences (Cheney 2007). Both the Western and the Ugandan central government models do not necessarily reflect the local context (social and cultural realities) under which childhood is shaped. In northern Uganda, for instance, many of the participants did not know their numeric age but rather defined their status in terms of "functionality" and "relationality" (Morrow 2013) as Chapter 2 elaborates.

Reconstruction programs and processes implementation are grounded in mainstream dominant guidelines, which are also under the guidance of the Ugandan central government's frameworks. The numeric age perspective, for instance, determines who falls under the categories of children and youth hence their access to and use of designated humanitarian assistance goods and services. This excludes some members of the community who do not self-identify as their age suggests given the roles they perform and community members they closely relate with. This was, however, not surprising to the humanitarian project implementers who were aware of this dilemma but choose to follow formal protocol for the sake of funding. One key informant, an employee with an NGO explains:

> Not everyone knows their age but if proposals are to be accepted, especially for funding, clarity over who is targeted is required. The best way to show that is using age groups, which we transplant from government documents...it is good because it limits duplication of services.

As described above, programs used normalized descriptions that do not necessarily reflect communal organization. They are "transplants" from government documents. Important to highlight, moreover, is that government documents are duplicates of the international documents. The government documents reflect the dominant understanding as a way of impressing the donors and receive funding. Smith (2012) notes that Uganda received USD 1.1 billion in humanitarian assistance between 2001 and 2010. The government and non-governmental organizations operating in the region therefore prioritize the funding requirements and specifications over the local concerns the communities might have. Communities are to the contrary organized in complex multifaceted ways that are not reflected by formal central government documents. Scholars argue that the neglect of communal organization is not an oversight but rather a strategy by the government. The government has, for instance, adopted the Western theorizing of young men as violent to justify the spending of a big portion of the aid on ammunition as a way of maintaining political stability (Brown 1997).

Reflecting on both protection and participation theories and the findings of this study, I argue that childhood in northern Uganda is complex and cannot be sufficiently discussed in binary constructions. Therefore, children need to have autonomy and thus decide on issues specifically affecting their lives. Using adults to discuss children's issues is limited and may ignore children-specific concerns hence calling for self-representation by children. Given their intersectional nature though, children also deserve to be treated as a special category facing the material effects of circumstances differently from adults. Children in post-conflict Uganda specifically occupy a position that is unique from other children in Uganda due to the war and the national child/adult binary that does not necessarily apply. They (children) thus need to be protected legally and socially to avoid further harm. In the post-conflict setting, children are described as adults due to the roles and responsibilities they hold hence the adult/child distinction blurred. However, government interventions are crucial to intervene and minimize the harmful encounters such children might face. I, therefore, settle with Hanson (2012)'s observation that "children's rights (and responsibilities) involve a double claim, including equal rights and special rights" (71). Hence acknowledging differences that make the difference between children and adults.

In addition, understanding childhood demands a shift beyond the rights discourse and comprehension of context-relevant social justice as a way of catering for the special needs of children. Since children under the Western and national frameworks are not automatically children in the indigenous understanding, rights need to be advocated with a clear understanding of the local construction, which informs children's everyday experiences.

While human rights activists appreciate that active involvement of young people is more ethical, children and youth participation in Uganda is still limited. In Soroti district, participation narratives were evident. The local community, however, did not use them in describing childhood. Rather protection, which incorporates provision and guidance, was applied in explaining childhood. Given the roles they perform, young people who participated actively in important communal activities were locally described as adults. Communities, for instance, treated the children who headed households in the same capacity as adults. Humanitarian assistance agencies nonetheless referred to them as child-headed households. The understanding of both childhood and adulthood is, in this case, reliant on roles and performativity. While scholars have critiqued the understanding of childhood in relation to adulthood, I still found it relevant in this study although with important limitations. This is because the ability to perform is measured based on locally standardized notions that disregard alternative notions of ability such as those performed by the differently abled bodies. This negatively impacts such bodies that might need care all the time since they would be categorized as inherently dependent and thus infantilized. Chapter 2 discusses the northern Uganda local understanding of childhood and how the dominant narrative has impacted this local view.

Conclusion

Understanding the constitution of childhood and youthhood, as well as other population categories' dynamics, demands positioning analysis within the social context in which such identities are actualized. The lived experiences of populations under study should thus inform such categorization. Since African societies are relational in nature (Christiansen et al. 2006), children and youth self-identification should be understood in relation to other community member perception of them. This volume in addition to young people's views, therefore, includes perceptions from community leaders and opinion leaders, as well as NGOs working with children and youth. This expounds on how young people position themselves in relation to how they are positioned by the society in which they reside and survive.

Generational categories including childhood, adulthood, and youth-hood are neither neutral nor natural (Christiansen et al. 2006). These categories are influenced by the desire for power and authority as well as status and belonging. One's identity, therefore, shifts depending on the circumstance at the time and in situations of armed violence, precedence is given to the identity that permits survival. In situations of distress, identities shift continually and "within the same day, a person can be positioned as child, youth and adult" (ibid.: 12). Young people in northern Uganda for instance were situated as (child) parents, students, daughters, and sons, former (child) soldiers, prostitutes, and wives among others. Childhood in this situation at times came along with privileges yet at times increased marginalization and dependency. Whatever permitted survival was adopted at that moment.

References

Abebe, T., & Ofusu-Kusi, Y. (2016). Beyond pluralizing African childhoods: Introduction. *Childhood, 23*, 303–316.

Africa Renew. (2013, May). Youth unemployment: Lessons from Ethiopia. https://www.un.org/africarenewal/magazine/may-2013/youth-unemployment-lessons-ethiopia.

Andrews, A. B., & Kaufman, N. H. (1999). *Implementing the UN convention on the rights of the child: A standard of living adequate for development.* London: Praeger.

Aries, P. (1962). *Centuries of childhood: A social history of family life.* New York: Vintage Books.

Bass, L. E. (2004). *Child labor in sub-Saharan Africa.* Boulder: Lynne Rienner.

Blattman, C., & Annan, J. (2009). Child combatants in northern Uganda: Reintegration myths and realities. In R. Muggah (Ed.), *Security and post-conflict reconstruction: Dealing with fighters in the aftermath of war* (pp. 103–126). New York, NY: Routledge.

Boakye-Boaten, A. (2010). Changes in the concept of childhood: Implications on children in Ghana. *Journal of International Social Research, 3*(10), 104–115.

Bourdillon, M. (2006). Children and work: A review of current literature and debates. *Development and Change, 37*(6), 1201–1226.

Boyden, J. (1997). Childhood and the policy makers: A comparative perspective on the globalization of childhood. In A. James & A. Pout (Eds.), *Constructing* and reconstructing childhood: Contemporary issues in the sociological study of childhood (2nd ed., pp. 190–215). London: Falmer Press.

Boyden, J., & de Berry, J. (2004). Children and youth on the front line: Ethnography, armed conflict and displacement. New York: Berghahn Books.

Brown, C. (1997). Universal human rights: A critique. The International Journal of Human Rights, 1(2), 41–65.

Cheney, K. (2007). Pillars of the nation: Child citizens and Ugandan national development. Chicago and London: The University of Chicago Press.

Chilisa, B. (2012). Indigenous research methodologies. London: Sage.

Christiansen, C., Utas, M., & Vigh, H. E. (Eds.). (2006). Navigating youth generating adulthood: Social becoming in an African context. Uppsala: Nordiska Afrikaninstitute.

Cunningham, H. (1995). Children and childhood in western society since 1500. Edinburgh: Pearson Education.

Dolan, C. (2009). Social torture: The case of northern Uganda, 1986–2006. New York and Oxford: Berghahn Books.

Fernando, C., & Ferrari, M. (2013). Handbook of resilience in children of war. New York: Springer.

Grier, B. (2006). Invisible hands: Child labor in colonial Zimbabwe. Portsmouth, NH: Heinemann.

Hanson, K. (2012). Schools of thought in children's rights. In M. Liebel (Ed.), Children's rights from below: Cross-cultural perspectives (pp. 63–79). New York and Hampshire: Palgrave Macmillan.

Harris-Short, S. (2003). International human rights law: Imperialist, inept and ineffective? Cultural relativism and the UN Convention on the rights of the child. Human Rights Quarterly, 25(1), 130–181.

Hendrick, H. (1997). Constructions and reconstructions of British childhood: An interpretative survey, 1800 to the present. In A. James & A. Prout (Eds.), Constructing and reconstructing childhood (pp. 34–62). London: Falmer Press.

Holt, J. C. (1994). Escape from childhood. New York: Dutton.

Howard, S. (Ed.) (2013). Childhood in Africa. An Interdisciplinary Journal, 3(1). 2009 ISSN 1948-6502.

Human Rights Watch. (2007). World report. New York. www.hrw.org.

Ignatieff, M. (2001). The attack on human rights. Foreign Affairs, 80(6), 102–116. Council on foreign relations.

Jenks, C. (1996). Childhood. London and New York: Routledge.

Jenks, C. (2009). Constructing childhood sociologically. In J. M. Kehily (Ed.), An introduction to childhood studies. Berkshire: Open University Press.

Johnny, L. (2006). Reconceptualizing childhood: Children's rights and youth participation in schools. International Education Journal, 7(1), 17–25.

Kehily, M. J. (2009). Understanding childhood: An introduction to some key themes and issues. In An introduction to childhood studies (pp. 1–17). Maidenhead: Open University Press.

Kendall, N. (2008). Vulnerability' in AIDS-affected states: Rethinking child rights, educational institutions, and development paradigms. *International Journal of Educational Development, 28,* 365–383.

Kilbride, P., & Kilbride, J. (1990). *Changing family life in East Africa: Women and children at risk.* University Park: The Pennsylvania State University Press.

Lawson, S. (1998). Democracy and the problem of cultural relativism, normative issues for international politics. *Global Society, 12*(2), 251–270.

Liebel, M. (2012). *Children's rights from below: Cross-cultural perspectives.* Palgrave Macmillan.

Machel, G. (2000, September). *The impact of armed conflict on children: A critical review of progress made and obstacles encountered in increasing protection for war-affected children.* The International Conference on War Affected Children, Winnipeg, Canada.

Mead, M., & Wolfenstein, M. (1954). *Childhood in contemporary cultures.* Chicago: Chicago University Press.

Mohanty, C. T. (2003). *Feminism without borders: Decolonizing theory practicing solidarity.* Durham and London: Duke University Press.

Morrow, V. (2011). *Understanding children and childhood* (Background Briefing Series No. 1). Lismore: Centre for Children and Young People, Southern Cross University.

Morrow, V. (2013). What's in a number? Unsettling the boundaries of age. *Childhood, 20,* 151–155. https://doi.org/10.1177/0907568213484199.

Mutiibwa, P. (1992). *Uganda since independence: A story of unfulfilled hopes.* Trenton: Africa World Press.

Namuggala, V. F. (2017). Gambling, dancing, sex work: Notions of youth employment in Uganda. *IDS Bulletin, 47*(3).

Nikku, B. R. (2012). Children's rights in disasters: Concerns for social work- insights from South Asia and possible lessons for Africa. *International Social Work, 56,* 51–66.

Nyerere, J. K. (1968). *Ujamaa-essays on socialism.* Dar-es-salaam: Oxford University Press.

Offit, T. (2008). *Conquistadores de la calle: Child street labor in Guatemala City.* Austin: University of Texas Press.

Oyewumi, O. (1998). Making history: Creating gender: Some methodological and interpretive questions in the writing of Oyo oral Traditions. *History in Africa, 25,* 263–305.

Panter-Brick, C., & Smith, T. M. (Eds.). (2000). *Abandoned children* (pp. 1–26). Cambridge: Cambridge University Press.

Panter-Brick, C., & Smith, T. M. (Eds.). (2004). *Abandoned children* (pp. 1–26). Cambridge: Cambridge University Press.

Pillay, J. (2014). Advancement of children's rights in Africa: A social justice framework for school psychologists. *School Psychology International, 35*(3), 225–240.

Reichert, E. (2006). Human rights: An examination of universalism and cultural relativism. *Journal of Comparative Social Welfare, 22*(1), 23–36.
Rousseau, S. (2011). Indigenous and feminist movements at the constituent Assembly in Bolivia: Locating the representation of indigenous women. *Latin American Research Review, 46*(2), 5–28.
Save the Children. (2006). *Children's rights: A teacher's guide.* London: Save the Children Fund.
Save the Children. (2017). *Stolen childhood: End of childhood report.*
Scheper-Hughes, N., & Sargent, C. F. (1998). *Small wars: The cultural politics of childhood.* Berkeley: University of California press.
Sewpaul, V., & Matthais, C. (2013). Editorial. *International Social Work, 56*(1), 3–6.
Sjoberg, L. (2013). *Gendering global conflict: Toward a feminist theory of war.* New York: Columbia University Press.
Sjoberg, L. (2014). *Gender, war and conflict.* Cambridge: Polity Press.
Smith, A. B. (2002). Interpreting and supporting participation rights: Contributions from sociocultural theory. *The International Journal of Children's Rights, 10*(1), 73–88.
Smith, K. (2012). *Global humanitarian assistance: Uganda. Resources for crisis response, vulnerability and poverty eradication.* Global Humanitarian Assistance, A Development Initiative.
Spitzer, H., & Twikirize, J. (2013). War affected children in northern Uganda: No easy path to normality. *International Social Work, 56,* 67–79.
Stasiulis, D. (2002). The active child citizen: Lessons from Canadian policy and the children's movement. *Citizenship Studies, 6,* 507–537.
Swadener, B. B., Kabiru, M., & Njenga, A. (2000). *Does the village still raise the child? A collaborative study of changing child-rearing and early education in Kenya.* Albany: State University of New York Press.
UNICEF. (2005). *Childhood under threat. The state of the world's children 2005.* https://www.unicef.org/sowc05/english/childhooddefined.html.
United Nations. (1989). *Convention on the rights of the child.* Retrieved from http://www.childrensrights.ie/sites/default/files/UNCRCEnglish.pdf.
Wall, J. (2008). Human rights in light of childhood. *International Journal of Children's Rights, 16,* 523–543.
Wane, J. (2011). African indigenous feminist thought. In *The politics of cultural knowledge* (pp. 7–21). New York: Springer.
Wane, N. N. (2013). (Re)claiming indigenous knowledge: Challenges, resistance, and opportunities. *Decolonization: Indigeneity, Education and Society, 2*(1), 93–107.
War Child. (2015, June 16). *The reality of child-headed households: Northern Uganda study.* A longitudinal study on the affect of income generating activity on education and protection outcomes for children and child headed households in northern Uganda.

CHAPTER 4

Local Perceptions of Childhood, Youthhood, and Adulthood

INTRODUCTION

This chapter continues and deepens issues raised in the first two chapters through a discussion of population categorization in war-torn regions with focus on northern Uganda. It provides alternative understandings to numeric age in the form of what childhood scholars have termed "functional" and "relational" age (Morrow 2013) drawing on experiences of formerly displaced communities. In this chapter, I argue that childhood in war-torn regions demands context-specific analysis. Such childhoods are not only different from Western mainstream constructions but also culturally and situationally constructed differently. Formalized frameworks often cannot accommodate population categories in fragile situations. At times, childhood in conflict situations also challenges local cultural notions of childhood, hence creating a kind of childhood that is different from the pre-conflict understanding. Children in war-torn situations therefore are positioned in contradiction to cultural, national, and international expectations relating to childhood. This creates such children as a unique category deserving special attention, which they are rarely accorded. The support provided to children in most cases fails to appreciate this intricate position they embody and instead forces them to suit predetermined expectations and frameworks.

This chapter emphasizes that there is no single understanding of childhood, but rather various childhoods grounded in sociocultural perspectives. Sociocultural narratives are, however, also not fixed. The chapter thus explores the dynamism in constructions of childhood focusing on transformations of local childhood perspectives influenced by the war comparing pre-conflict and post-conflict communal perceptions of children and childhood. This chapter also brings out childhood as a gendered construct by discussing differentiated expectations, experiences and roles performed by children as gendered beings.

This chapter concludes that universalistic notions of childhood have limited applicability to the local experiences of children in fragile states. These notions, however, inform national approaches to childhood thus rendering them less applicable to war-affected children. It is thus crucial to clarify what we are really looking for when studying children especially in the case of Africa if a true representation of children's lived realities is to be made. Such analysis should strategically incorporate Global South understandings of both childhood and adulthood with local social and cultural systems and structures.

Western informed frameworks fail to capture the multifaceted nature of life formerly displaced communities embody thus hindering their access to and use of humanitarian assistance. Such persons manifest multidimensional identities that cannot be compartmentalized in restrictive, formal understandings in the form of children, youth, and adults since they are interconnected and shift from one category to another depending on the situation. Individuals cannot be fixed to singular categorical descriptions based on age. Despite scholarly criticism over the failed analysis of childhood as an independent category (Cheney 2011), childhood in northern Uganda is locally understood in relation to adulthood. To reflect local perspectives, I discuss these two aspects in relation to each other with a transitional phase commonly described as the youth. Before this deeper analysis, I wish to explore briefly why it is crucial to focus on African centered knowledge, which the following section presents.

Reframing Knowledge from an African Perspective

This chapter problematizes universalistic dominant knowledge systems and adopts a deconstructionist and decolonial approach to reframe what we know from an African perspective. This localized approach challenges the imposition of contextually inapplicable concepts to the postwar reconstruction of indigenous communities in northern Uganda. I provide a counter-narrative to the dominant view of childhood and youthhood by making a comparison between the northern Uganda informed understanding of the stages of human development, and the standardized universal constructions that have generally informed the development, reconstruction and recovery processes. I thus discuss the contradictions between the two perspectives in relation to their understandings of childhood and adulthood, and youthhood. The chapter further acknowledges that culture is not fixed, but rather dynamic and changing due to the impact of external factors including war, displacement, encampment, and globalization as well as historical processes like colonialism. To assess cultural dynamism in northern Uganda, this chapter compares the pre-conflict and post-conflict local understanding of childhood examining the impact the war has created for such local constructions.

The concepts "children" and "adult" are applicable and locally relevant to northern Uganda (although contextually different). There is, however, no concrete evidence of cultural applicability of the concept of youth. The concept is largely used by humanitarian and government agencies compared to the local populace. It is therefore difficult for the local community to relate to the concept in culturally relevant ways. However, due to lack of an alternative term, the concept youth is used in this volume to refer to the human phase of development that involves changing and crossing over from childhood to adulthood. This phase of human growth does not have specific numeric age brackets. Adopting such an understanding aids my integration of culture and context-dependent interpretation of social reality in northern Uganda's formerly displaced communities, while at the same time capturing the universal understanding of growth and development (numeric age bracket) used by the formal perspective adopted by the national and international policies and programs implemented in the region.

Young people in situations of armed violence reflect all the tenets of children presented by the different theories discussed in the previous chapter. Children for instance need to be protected from harmful circumstances and provided for with basic needs. They are thus vulnerable and susceptible to victimization and need to be protected legally and socially to avoid extreme harm. Children at the same time are actively involved as social beings and due to war situations are exposed to adult roles and responsibilities earlier in life than would be expected in normal settings. Such exposures include sexual encounters due to rape and abduction, headship of households due to death of parents and separation especially in the process of displacement and encampment. These result in abandonment of children and break down of child protecting cultural systems for instance the extended family structure, which traditionally caters for orphans and vulnerable children. Such experiences distort the child/adult binaries, which humanitarian programs heavily rely upon.

Given the roles and responsibilities children embrace during displacement in the post-conflict setting, they are "adultized" by the local communities hence the adult/child distinction is blurred. This creates a distinction between the communal perception and the government notions relating to childhood. It is therefore important to appreciate that children's rights simultaneously involve both equal rights and special rights (Liebel 2012). Understanding childhood therefore demands a shift beyond the rights discourse and comprehension of context-relevant social justice as a way of catering for the special needs of children. Since children under the Western and national frameworks are not automatically children in the indigenous understanding, rights need to be advocated with clear understanding of the local construction, which informs children's everyday experiences.

Contextualizing Childhood in Northern Uganda

In northern Uganda, both protection and participation approaches apply concurrently for children in the returned communities. This volume therefore adopts a multi-perspectival intersectional approach. That is to say, children's experiences do not have to be understood in specified rigid categorizations of either protection/vulnerable versus participation/agency. Rather, children's experiences are fluid depending on circumstances and at times multilayered in complex ways. For instance, children may experience contradicting occurrences simultaneously. Formerly displaced girls for instance are both vulnerable and thus in need of protection from sexual exploitation including defilement and rape, and early and forced marriages yet they can be actively involved in decision-making. While (early) marriages hinder children's rights to a "good" childhood, at times it is a survival strategy that children and their families have to take on. Marriage provides an alternative strategy to deal with limited access to resources including food and land, expands family connections and breeds peace. Marriage is thus simultaneously disempowering yet empowering too, depending on one's standpoint of view. Simply pathologizing marriage fails to appreciate the alternative viewpoints that inform such decisions.

Children have demonstrated resilience and agency by heading households and earning income to sustain themselves and at times their siblings. Children elaborated that they work (for pay) in both the private and public settings. The roles children perform are largely gendered to reflect social expectations. The boys are involved in income generating activities like brick laying, casual labor like fetching water, acting as watchmen (security guards) and hawking. Girls on the other hand are more dominant in feminized roles including babysitting, and housekeeping. There are also activities that involve both boys and girls for instance roadside vending. Both boys and girls carry buckets and boxes selling bottled water, soda, and juices, others sell roast meat, chicken, plantain, cassava, and potatoes. Such jobs bring in daily income, and permit networking and independence. It is, however, tasking as it involves running after cars to sell to travelers, enduring bad weather and risking being involved in work-related accidents.

Research also shows that children and youth have reframed their understanding of work and employment to accommodate legally and socially unacceptable forms of income generation. They participate in prostitution, drug dealing and sports betting among other things (Namuggala 2017). Such notions of work problematize formalized notions of employment and official government frameworks that encourage agriculture. Formerly displaced young people lack skills and resources (including land) to effectively take on agricultural production hence adopting quick income generating strategies amidst critics from the older generation.

It is a children's right to be given space to voice their experiences and concerns, and where possible be involved in decision-making, with their views being given due weight. But, because they are not fully developed as adults, they at the same time need to be protected from harm, including exploitative and hazardous child labor, sexual exploitation and child soldiering among other things. It is, therefore, necessary to recognize differences that make the difference between adults and children if children's rights are to be sustainably attained. Appreciating differences also involve acknowledging the experiences of individual children within the broad category of children. For instance, while young mothers are universally vulnerable, unmarried young mothers in northern Uganda were locally identified as an especially vulnerable category within the broad category due to lack of basic needs and social support. A single mother of two noted:

> When you are married, your husband respects you because your family knows him, the people know you have the blessing of the parents and the clan leaders, they love you and support you in case of anything for instance if a child is sick… just having children (without being married) can however, even lead to misery. Men responsible can neglect their responsibility.

Mothering is culturally a good thing. It is, however, expected to happen following the right procedure, which involves bride price payment. When this is not done, the result is single parenthood and the responsibility of raising the child heavily relies on the mother. Raising children as single teenage mothers is so challenging that it exposes girls to more exploitation sexually and economically as they struggle to provide for their children. Single parenting is also socially demeaning since the local community stigmatizes it to imply lack of integrity and self-respect on the side of the girl. The girl's family may also feel this negative impact through labeling and stigmatization. The special needs of young mothers are therefore likely to be disregarded hence affecting services for such categories of the population and consequently worsening their vulnerability.

Contradictions Between Mainstream Western and Local Indigenous Constructions of Childhood

There is no single agreed upon understanding of a child or childhood that fully represents the various conditions children encounter. There are also differences in the understanding of critical concepts that define childhood, including vulnerability, ability, protection, agency, and family. Such differences feature within, between and among groups. This section explores the major issues that contribute to such contradictions including age, child labor, sexuality and gender as critical aspects of analysis. In conceptualizing childhoods, a dichotomous binary has emerged between the "ideal" developed world childhood and the "other" unfulfilled childhood of the Global South. This section highlights the distinctive features that inform this binary construction, examining how they have impacted the reconstruction phase in northern Uganda.

The dominant Western understanding of childhood assumes a linear progression from childhood to adulthood resulting in normative constructions of "right" and "wrong" ages for children's participation in "adult activities," including paid and unpaid employment, and marriage (Morrow 2010). This understanding has informed universal declarations on children and childhood that are globally employed to structure policies and programs targeting children. According to childhood scholar Morrow (2013), linear constructions of childhood create a sense of failure in cases where children fail to conform to the expected linear progression. It is therefore prudent to contextualize notions of childhood to reflect the local realities that children experience on a daily basis rather than imposing externally informed frameworks that may not capture locally relevant circumstances. Standardized notions over pressurize the children to follow the set linear progression. For instance, in literature relating to hegemonic masculinities, boys sometimes turn violent due to failure to live to expected social and economic standards (Dolan 2009; Sommers 2006; Urdal 2004). Male children, youth (and men) in northern Uganda have fallen victim to such theorization, resulting in them being labeled as violent in relation to female youth and women who are labeled victims.

The linear progression in stages of human development as conceptualized in the mainstream frameworks relies on numeric age to determinant of childhood, youthhood and adulthood. At the age of eighteen (18), in many societies, childhood ends and adulthood immediately sets in, which calls for individual responsibility legally and financially (Morrow 2011). Numeric age is thus understood in relation to individuals. In sub-Saharan Africa, however, numeric age categorization is highly contested due to limited applicability given the circumstances (Bourdillon 2006). Research demonstrates that, both children and parents "very often, do not know their numeric age, or their dates of birth. They don't talk in terms of specific numeric age, but what they can do" (Morrow 2013: 152). In northern Uganda, participants elaborated that adulthood is attained through a process that involves fulfillment of socially expected practices including construction of a hut at the parents' house to demonstrate the ability to provide shelter to one's children. One key informant explained that maturity follows some criteria, i.e.:

> Someone who is ready for marriage i.e. one who can have children (potentiality) and one in position to establish his own house but around the parents' house… every child/youth of reproductive age has a hut at their parent's home. It's a sign of your maturity.

The transition from childhood to adulthood is a process not for the individual solely but rather a family and communal venture. Adulthood in northern Uganda thus involves community endorsement of one's maturity. Using one's numeric age to determine individual adulthood is thus limiting in this context.

In addition to numeric understanding, the concept "age" also implies "functional and relational age" (Morrow 2013: 151) which this study found to resonate more with northern Uganda. To varying degrees, children's status and roles are marked not by numeric age, but by the kinds of everyday tasks they perform and/or are expected to perform in their respective societies. In some parts of India for instance, functional age is demonstrated in how much rice one can cook, while Ethiopian communities look at how much coffee and Injera (bread) one can make (Morrow 2013). In addition to cooking abilities, in northern Uganda functionality also is determined by how many siblings one can efficiently care for in the absence of parents. Especially significant for this study is the gendered construction of adulthood through the feminization of such division of labor socially. Marriage and childbirth transition such functionality to adulthood. In relation to this, one female respondent explained that,

> When a girl can cook especially atapa (a local delicacy meal made from millet flour mixed with boiling water), and does not get burnt, when she can take good care of her siblings – bathe them, feed them and maintain the house. Then she is ready for marriage because those are signs that she can take care of her own house and children.

While performing such roles is crucial, the ability to perform them only means adulthood when combined with marriage and or childbirth as a public display and approval of one's maturity. Practicing such roles in a marriage relation is what culminates in adulthood. Relationality is not static but rather varies according to situation. For instance, relating with mothers and wives in similar capacities, i.e. with children and husbands, respectively, elevates young women to womanhood status in the community even when not formerly married. In northern Uganda, it is expected that once one becomes a mother, they relate with other mothers for guidance and direction. Irrespective of their biological age, such girls cease to be or even relate (in the capacity of children) with children. In a female only FGD, youth explained that,

4 LOCAL PERCEPTIONS OF CHILDHOOD, YOUTHHOOD, AND ADULTHOOD

> It is known all over when you get your own (biological) child, then you stop being a child, because a child cannot have a child. You stop to play games with children, and become "decent" and serious with life. If you do not change your conduct, other mothers sit you down. It is like you are shaming them and their position/status in community. It also means you are a disgrace to the child you gave birth to.

Another respondent noted,

> When you get a child, your name changes, you are someone's mother. You now start being addressed making references to your child...the mother of (so and so...) It is a sign of respect from the community. Most women are called by their first born's names, dead or alive, to mark it as a turning point in young women's lives.

Being hailed in ways that evoke motherhood is a constant reminder to young mothers about their new attained identity as well as consequential roles and responsibilities. Child mothers in this case have to give up their childhood(s) for that of their children, and the motherhood status in order to fit in communally set frameworks. The local understanding does not reflect the concept of "child mothers" as applied by humanitarian and other external frameworks. Locally one can only be either a mother or a child but not both. A mother in relation to one's child and a child in relation to one's parents. One cannot be a "child mother" in the way it is perceived by reconstruction programs as a state of being "a child with a child". Having children automatically and permanently changes a girl's sense of identity and belonging (even if the born child dies) and automatically creates some kind of policing within and among individuals as a way of safeguarding the honor and integrity of the motherhood status. In this case, adulthood is thus determined through childbirth. When asked about how old they were a number of participants counted at the number of births. "She is grown, she is a mother of three", one respondent described another. This directly links to the understanding of someone who has children as an adult and vice vasa unless other circumstances are at play including barrenness. One male elder explained that,

> A child is someone who does not have a child yet, someone who has not yet brought another human being into this world. Such a person cannot understand some things... The ability to have a child changes who you

are – you become related to another family right away, how you think and what you do all change! Being a mother makes you think about the consequences of your actions to the entire community, clan and family.

This quote identifies what I term "demonstrated ability" as a contributing factor to agency and vulnerability. Children are termed vulnerable because they have not yet demonstrated their ability to do some things that are deemed important by society. Barrenness is also a marker of vulnerability since it is an expression of failure to demonstrate ability to add to community population. During the research, several participants emphasized that some circumstances can only be understood and reflected upon when one experiences them, because lived experience is irreversible. In this perspective, the local understanding of vulnerability implicates the body by evoking "feeling" as a critical concept of transition from childhood to adulthood. While feeling is individualistic in nature, it has to be attributed to a communal cause. While children are born to individuals, they are part of a collective group, i.e. family, clan, and community.

Feeling is, in addition, a gendered construct. Childbirth and childrearing as a determinant of adulthood heavily applies to women. For instance, women are generally culturally solely blamed for the inability to conceive. While the number of children tells how old a woman is, and thus conveys her expected level of maturity, the same is not true for males because they can have several wives and many children even at an early age. For boys and young men, marriage marks adulthood. The number of women a man has paid bride price for and how well he provides for them and their children demonstrates the level of maturity and respect he commands in the community.

Life events also determine social location within the community. Such events provide landmarks used in telling life stories and deriving meaning out of them. At the same time, humanitarian programs use such events to estimate the numeric age of the particular individuals as a way of categorizing them. Also, events provided a rough idea of people's ages during general population counting and registration. This made events such crucial elements in the lives of the returning populations. Important as events are, many for the returning communities were soaked in pain and negative memories that some distanced themselves from these lifetime events. Nevertheless, they provide an alternative approach to understanding age, which is not reflected in numeric, functional, and relational age descriptions. When asked her age, one respondent pointed to a small girl aged about three years and said:

> I was about that size when we were moved into the camp. My mother carried me on her back all the way…By that time the rebels had attacked the school taking away many girls who never returned. I remember everything! You don't know how people died…my dad too. We had no protection but the camp.

Further probing clarified that this respondent referred to the abduction at St. Mary's college boarding school, Aboke, in 1996. The rebels attacked this girls' school and took 139 girls (Temmerman 2001). This abduction was largely publicized in the media. So many stakeholders would easily remember when it was referenced. While such information may suffer limited authenticity due to memory issues, the events help individuals relate with others in their generation as well as normative constructions reflected in age. If the respondent in the above quote was 3 in 1996 when they moved to the camp, then it could be estimated that by 2015, when this research was conducted, this young lady was 22 years old and thus a youth.

Generational tracking is one other way parents and the general community keeps track of their children. Identifying with the same generational cohort demonstrates one's growth and development and (in)ability to fulfill certain roles. One female clan member noted: "When all your child's childhood friends are married and have children, it triggers you to find out what's wrong with yours (children)", in case they are not progressing in a similar direction. While such understanding is important for community evaluation, it creates pressure for the youth to keep on track with expected social relations. The pressure, however, is not as linear as the numeric age description. This local narrative provides alternatives for instance; you may have a child, be married or have both. Nonetheless, societal expectations may hinder individual aspirations that children might have, which may not be reflected in the societal progression trends.

Another distinction in definitions of children relates to individualism and collectiveness. Dominant Western constructions define children as individuals that form separate entities as citizens within nation states (Cheney 2007). In Uganda (as in much of Africa), however, children are understood in relation to communities, tribes, families, and clans.

Understanding childhood goes beyond the individual children to include the community in form of parents, leaders, teachers, elders, and ancestors (Boyden and de Berry 2004; Swadener et al. 2000). Nonetheless, Africa has not been exempted from global frameworks. Interventions by international aid programs targeting orphans (Cheney 2010), child soldiers (Wessels 2006) and the girl child (Kendall 2010), have transformed traditional family relations toward more individualistic tendencies. In northern Uganda, agencies utilize individualistic approaches in dealing with individual children in schools, and health services. Spitzer and Twikirize (2013) for instance highlight the medicalization of psychosocial support for individual child soldiers that ignore the role of the family and the community with which these children interact. This results in the stigmatization of such children by the community, which hinders their social reintegration. Communities in Soroti attested to this problem by explaining that former child soldiers were problematic and parents discouraged their children from interacting with them. This stigmatization resulted in isolation, thereby halting former child soldiers' acceptance back into the community. One way such stigmatization could be avoided is by involving other community members in programs previously solely intended for child soldiers—for instance providing programs that cater for all community children, the majority of whom suffer from poverty, malnutrition, and disease.

In northern Uganda, the community also upholds collective responsibility for what elsewhere might be construed as individual actions. An entire group may be judged based on the socially and culturally unbecoming acts of one individual. For instance, respondents highlighted that if one (child) mother misbehaves in relation to social expectations, then community generalizes such conduct to all mothers. Collectivization is also true for youth. Due to a handful of youth who used to go to nightclubs, and were involved in violence, the youth accrued a negative connotation from the community consequently leading to distancing themselves from the category youth. Such conditions place significant pressure on individuals to live up to the social expectations due to collective responsibilities and also collective consequences. For instance, women as a group employ measures to control socially unacceptable behavior among individual women and/or mothers. "Sitting you down" as the earlier quote suggested, is one of the strategies women adopt to safeguard their position in society. It is a serious intervention by socially respected women. These have a good record in marriage with no divorce, have had and/or raised a good number of children in a socially accepted way. "Sitting down" therefore has experienced women draw on their experiences to rebuke, counsel and at times punish others for misconduct. One participant emphasized the fact that, "they put sense in you!" The "sense" such elders impart into young mothers is intended to emphasize the new roles and responsibilities that come with mothering, focusing on change of identity irrespective of one's age and maintaining the status quo of mothers and/or wives. Therefore, childhood in northern Uganda is not an abstract concept but rather a reflection on particular bodies impacted by gender, feeling, and ability in relation to other social categories, structures and systems. Emphasizing individualized approaches in addressing children's issues hinders the applicability and thus relevancy of programs intended for reconstructing war-torn regions.

Shifting Safety Zones

Both dominant and indigenous constructions of childhood acknowledge location as a critical feature for child development. Children are expected to be in private and not public spaces unless under adult supervision, such as in schools. While studies about "street children" have demonstrated that such children are agentic, independent, and at times happier to work and/or live on the street (Offit 2008), dominant narratives term them vulnerable and victimized. As such frameworks promote forcing children to leave the streets as a way of protecting them from danger (Kendall 2010). Contrary to dominant assumptions and pre-conflict constructions that emphasized communal and collective raising of children in homes, post-conflict northern Uganda indicated that homes sometimes are not the best places for childhood development given instances of drug abuse and alcohol abuse, domestic violence, early and forced marriages especially after the war. When asked whether he had participated in any form of violence, one 22-year-male youth answered,

> Yes, I fought with my father when I was sixteen and as a result he chased me from home. I beat him for beating my mother. He used to come back home drunk and fought every night. He always battered my mother and on that fateful night I had gone to stop him, them he turned on me. I felt it was enough. I was more energetic so I managed to control him.

Mothers and their children in violent families live under constant fear and abuse and the street, with all its difficulties, seems to provide a somewhat better alternative. While battered women and children in the developed world may have domestic violence shelters (Goodmark 2008), those in Uganda, Africa and many other parts of the developing world do not have such options. Emphasizing the role of the family and the domestic space in upbringing of children therefore as does the dominant narrative, fails to acknowledge the unique circumstances encountered by children living in less privileged regions of the world like northern Uganda. During the war, families were targets of the rebels for abductions. Children and their families moved to city centers in the evenings in search for safety in what has been termed "night commuters". Instead of being the safe zone, the private space became the danger zone. Also during the displacement, some children lost their parents thus becoming orphaned or unaccompanied minors. Such children have no families to turn to. What this means is that circumstances and context should inform post-conflict reconstruction programming.

Besides physical abuse in domestic spaces in return areas, some returned child soldiers suffer rejection from their families and communities and hence find the street, where they work as sex workers and hawkers, more comforting. This shows that the traditionally understood family structure is not always achievable for children in various contexts, especially in fragile and broken societies like those in conflict and post-conflict situations. As such, if children are to be reintegrated successfully, context-specific analysis is inevitable. The voices of the children as well as their experiences must be acknowledged and normative constructions of both childhood and children, and critical concepts like the family should be deconstructed. Children's voices are embedded in the experiences they have. These experiences are however multidimensional given the gender, location, parenthood and marriage statuses among other identity markers hence the need for an intersectional approach to childhood.

Intersectionality and Childhood

Childhood scholars, drawing on the sociocultural perspective elaborate that expectations of attaining adulthood are gendered. For example, "girls are generally considered adults once they reach puberty, while boys are considered adults when they finish school, begin to make their own money, leave for work or get married" (Kendall 2010: 32). In such circumstances, gender intersects with social class to impact childhood. The poor who cannot afford higher education attain maturity faster than the average class that stays in school longer. In Uganda, childhood is not only gendered but also regionally determined with the northern part of the country having higher school dropout rates compared to the southern region (UNICEF 2014). Girls are particularly disadvantaged further due to cultural constructions that breed sons' preference. In situations of limited resources and services including education and health, preference is given to the boy child. To highlight this, one local leader explains the gendered bias in access to educational services,

> We still have a lot of work to do as leaders, as community. Our community needs to value education for all children. Parents just need an excuse to pull the girl out of school. Some are married off, others are sent to Kampala to work as house girls (house maids) and others keep at home to help with housework.

The limited education of the girl child works hand in hand with her involvement in both paid and unpaid labor activities (domestic and public). In some cases, girl children are made to work as domestic workers, what is commonly referred to as "house girls" in order to raise school fees for their brothers (Namuggala 2015). In Uganda, child labor is a serious contentious issue since it interferes with other rights to which children are entitled including education. I thus find it important to elaborate more on child labor as a contrasting feature of childhood between the Western and the non-Western world.

Despite Uganda having free basic education policies, i.e. Universal Primary Education (UPE) and Universal Secondary Education (USE), some parents are reluctant to take children to school. It is even worse in post-conflict situations and northern Uganda still lags behind in education (Bird and Higgins 2009; UNICEF 2005). This is due to limited educational infrastructure, resources and systems, limited personnel, and perpetual absenteeism from teachers (Bird and Higgins 2009). To counter this situation, legal and punitive measures have been adopted through government institutions like the police to encourage child education and also minimize child labor. Yet I observed that the local community did not positively view the use of force in frameworks such as the law and the legal system. Threatening the communities with imprisonment due to failure to send children to school for instance exacerbated the negative local perceptions of the government programs. The local population perceived the government as being against working for them hence limiting their cooperation with government programs. Understanding why parents marry off school going children and changing their attitudes in that aspect might provide a lasting solution rather than imprisoning them for doing so. This is because it strains relations between the systems and structures and the local population, yet at the same time affects the children it intends to protect. For instance, having parents imprisoned or compensate financially for wrong actions reduces the amount of money available for domestic supplies which affects children.

Child Laboring for Survival

Child labor is yet another significant point of departure and contradiction between Western and non-Western constructions of childhood. Child labor is conceptualized as "any form of work which deprives children of their childhood, their potential and dignity, and is harmful to physical and mental development" (Khakshour et al. 2015: 468). Such work denies children opportunities to attend school, prompts them to leave school prematurely or attempt to combine school attendance with long and heavy work, which is in most cases harmful to their development. This understanding is based on the assumption that school is readily available for children and is more important for their health and survival. In war-torn regions like northern Uganda however, educational infrastructure, resources, systems and staff are compromised (Bird and Higgins 2009).

Childhood in the "Western world has become increasingly institutionalized and the school/work divide has become more sharply drawn" (Morrow 2010: 437). In this perspective, work, and education are termed unharmonious, therefore, children should not be permitted to work until they finish their education. In northern Uganda however, participants perceived education, as one other skill children have to acquire in their transition to adulthood. From the local perspective, the knowledge attained from formal education is inferior to the knowledge they require for survival in everyday life (see Invernizzi 2003). Children cannot, therefore, solely pursue education since it cannot efficiently satisfy adulthood requirements in the local Ugandan context. In addition, there are crosscutting roles between the private and the public space; for instance, a continuation of private roles at schools. Going to school is thus one among the other things children do.

In the context of sub-Saharan Africa, child labor is a very tricky undertaking. Preventing poor children from working is often harmful to them since they work to acquire the basic needs of food and clothing (Bass 2004) in addition to education requirements. Several participants elaborated that children have no choice but to work because they must fulfill school requirements in addition to helping to sustain their families.

In sub-Saharan Africa, working is a core component of the socialization process (Boakye-Boaten 2010) and thus a system of initiation into adulthood. Findings indicate that some children are household heads, which makes child laboring inevitable (War Child 2015). In Uganda specifically, child labor has been constructed and socially understood as a family support venture that affirms a sense of unity and belonging. In an indigenous Ugandan paradigm, children working especially within families is perceived as an ongoing training relevant for community survival and identity. Failure of parents to train their children in culturally relevant skills is thus termed betrayal and sabotage in the children's transition into adulthood. Children who lack this form of orientation find survival hard as adults. One clan leader expounds on work for children,

> Making your children not to work is the worst thing any parent can do for their children. That's promoting laziness! Who survives in the world without working? How? Tell me. We all have to work and our children should work right from a young age to develop such skills. The earlier you learn to work, the easier it gets in adulthood.

According to this participant, stopping children from working is a disfavor to both the children and society. The skills children attain are used for survival as adults and thus failure to have these skills creates misfits in society. Such children cannot fully identify with their local communities if they cannot perform socially expected roles. Communities therefore blame not only the individual child but also the family that raised the child. In another discussion, the participant makes a comparative assessment between education and work. She elaborates:

> Education is good? For who? The government? I tell you many of our children don't go further to qualify for educated people's jobs. Now if they also don't train for the substance survival work, they end up in-between and half baked, unable to do both...The only thing we have control over is our children and we shall continue doing what we believe is right as parents.

The argument is that even education trains people to work. In the situation of northern Uganda, however, many of the children do not attain required qualifications to be able to obtain "educated people's jobs". If they are to work therefore, they need to have the locally relevant skills, which are attained during childhood. It is thus inevitable for children in this region of the world to work or else they fail in life.

While work is crucial, the young generation has missed out on this essential aspect of socialization due to the displacement and encampment, which cultivated idleness and laziness. Idleness in the camp greatly affected children and youth. Young people thus have a difficult time integrating into the community because of the work-free childhood they had in the camp. Because youth lack the necessary survival skills, they resort to criminal and violent activities. This in turn reproduces assumptions in theories like the youth bulge theory that defines poor young men as violent. Dominant universal frameworks, therefore, recreate the negative connotations such frameworks have on the developing world and its people.

As a way of challenging child labor, some humanitarian agencies asserted that emphasizing the right to play was ideal for children's proper development and upbringing. In the Western context, play is a regulated activity with specified time as well as particular toys marked for specific ages and gender (Panter-Brick and Smith 2004). In northern Uganda's context, especially given the heavy workload returned communities have, play does not require allocated time because children can play during work time. One married mother of seven with two deceased children bitterly expressed her discontent with fronting play as critical for children.

> What is the importance of playing when you sleep hungry? Or maybe I should say can you play when you are hungry? All the bushes are overgrown, we have no food and you talk about play? That's not our problem... I have not heard, all my life, of a child who died because of not

playing. But I have witnessed children die of hunger. They (NGOs and government) say playing is about exercising but working is, too! You just honestly cannot set time aside for play... Children play as they work for instance on their way to the well, they go playing with each other.

In hunger- and poverty-stricken regions, play is perceived as a luxury activity and some local community members believe it should not be a center of discussion since the returned communities still had a lot to deal with as they resettled back into their lands. Giving children playtime also has gendered implications. Women work with their children to accomplish domestic chores so freeing the children, especially the girls, affects the women. As such, girls who do most of the domestic chores rarely get playtime.

The International Labor Organization (ILO) called for a total end to child labor by 2016 (Morrow 2010), it is however, important to reflect on regions like Africa where the ability to perform certain roles permits one into adulthood, creates a sense of identity and belonging. Animal rearing and agriculture for instance, according to the ILO, qualify as hazardous to children and may also affect children's education yet these are a survival mechanism for communities in northern Uganda. Denying children such skills is likely to deny them sociocultural respect, thus affecting their reintegration in the community. Emphasizing education is good, but in sub-Saharan Africa, it is not readily feasible given limited access to schools. In addition, formal education does not yield expected returns due to high levels of unemployment (Africa Renew 2013; Ayele et al. 2017). Involving children in informal sectors seems an appropriate strategy to produce job creators rather than seekers. Equipping children with socially relevant skills in addition to the formal education would also be appropriate. This might however, be overwhelming for the children.

Reframing Young People's Vulnerability

Another feature that complicates constructions of childhood is the concept vulnerability. According to the protection theorists, all children are deemed vulnerable by virtue of their numeric age. However, children's vulnerability in war-torn northern Uganda is reflected in the inability to fulfill certain roles and responsibilities, and make important communal networks especially outside the family. Such publically demonstrated ability determines the relations particular bodies can forge with others in the society, the social status they attain and the respect and entitlement they enjoy within large communal frameworks. Limited communal involvement thus poses a unique form of vulnerability for the children. The formerly displaced communities largely agree that young age par se does not automatically amount to vulnerability but the circumstances that surround birth of individual children do, i.e. some children are more vulnerable than others even within situations of violence. For instance children who are cursed, and those born out of extremely unpleasant circumstances, are the most vulnerable. This is explained by their limited social networks as some community members perceived them as being a social threat to harmony. Such children do not need protection from harm as much as others need, and instead other children to be protected from the harm the vulnerable can spread. One mother desperately spoke about her son born out of rape by a stranger:

> ...his rapist father brought [sexual bondage] upon me and my child. It [the curse] is following him. He is only 8 years yet he defiles girls younger than him. All parents around here hate him; they don't want him to play with their children [both boys and girls]. The boys fear he will teach them his bad behavior yet for the girls that he might rape them.... I have tried to help him but elders tell me the curse could have only been broken before the child was born but because I was living in the camp, I could not contact the healers for cleansing. When the child is born, the spirit is free and roaming, that it becomes very hard to contain it...

This terribly concerned mother believes her son is bearing a curse resulting from the rape. While she has other nine (9) dependents including young siblings and cousins, none of them has displayed that kind of conduct (i.e. sexual bondage as she terms it) which culturally strengthens her belief. In situations where the rapists are known, the child and mother can be handed over to the rapist or the rapist may be forced to marry his victim as a way of ending the curse. Locally it psychologically relieves the woman and the child of stigma, and improves communal perceptions of and relations with them. It also evokes the spiritual world as the solution. Taming the sexual harassment spirit cannot be done under normal circumstances but through a process of cleansing.

All this demonstrates how childhood constructions in Africa involve a wider community including the living and the dead, human, and non-human.

Other children who have suffered related discrimination are born to formerly abducted female youth. These are locally labeled "rebel children". Such young women's motherhood status resulted in pain instead of happiness because of the circumstances under which it happened. Rebels have caused disgrace to communities making it hard for civilian communities to accept such children as their own. Consequently children are labeled unworthy of communal love and protection. The community thus welcomed their daughters back from bandage but not the children they came along with.

Important to emphasize is that like childhood, vulnerability is not homogeneous. The local community in some aspects understands vulnerability differently from the dominant view, which brings out vulnerabilities that would not otherwise be considered important within dominant frameworks. There exists a daring need to understand the environment and communities in which affected individuals reside, as well as the past processes and events that have informed their contemporary situations. Universalizing approaches to vulnerability and childhood thus fails to capture experiences like that of the eight-year old discussed above. As a result, humanitarian programs fail to generate relevant approaches to encourage reintegration of such individuals.

The preceding discussion elaborated on the important contradictions between the mainstream Western understanding of childhood and the non-Western (northern Uganda) construction. These are further complicated by the war, encampment, and displacement in northern Uganda, which has transformed the traditional pre-conflict perspectives. Building sustainable peace therefore demands acknowledgment of such shifts in among other things forms of vulnerability, child labor, child marriages and other universalized forms of violence especially against children. Comparisons between hegemonic and alternative understandings of childhood present important divergences and contradictions, as well as intersections. This volume, however, also elaborates that childhood is not static but rather shifts in time and locations. In the following section, we address the impact war has had on children and local childhood constructions by comparing pre-conflict and post-conflict notions of childhood.

Pre-conflict versus Post-conflict Childhood in Northern Uganda

The war, displacement, and encampment have affected local perceptions of children, and childhood. While indigenous traditions still inform the local cultural conceptions of children, practical experiences within the communities do not entirely resonate with traditional expectations. For instance, the guardians, parents and clan leaders traditionally are expected to protect children from harm and mistreatment. Due to economic hardships, however, young people are exposed to child labor, early marriages, prostitution, and other forms of exploitation. The following discussion explores in detail.

Many aspects of childhood in contemporary sub-Saharan Africa no longer meet traditional expectations. This is due to external interactions including but not limited to colonialism and globalization. Scholars have noted that the fragmentation that exists between the southern and northern region of Uganda resulted from British colonial rule (Tornberg 2012). The British divide-and-rule policy produced ethnic marginalization that disfavored the northern tribes, and specifically women and children. These remained at home while the men were trained to be in the army. The southern region on the other hand took over administrative rule (HRW 2005; Mutiibwa 1992). Scholars observe that government has strategically used the northern Uganda conflict as a way of sustaining its power (Dolan 2009) through displacement and demobilization (Tornberg 2012). All this has resulted in the breakdown of social networks and socialization systems, hindering reintegration, and population categorization.

Globalization also plays a big role in affecting childhood standards as concepts are framed and reframed, changing in meaning and capacity in reference to global social complexes (Christiansen et al. 2006). Some respondents concluded that due to complex global developments, "children are no longer children". One leader explained that the availability of guns especially the small guns has tremendously transformed childhood. In his words,

> What can we do with these guns all over the place? The availability of guns is the biggest problem but do we manufacture guns in Uganda? No, they are outsiders who bring these things. There is a connection to the outside that we cannot even explain. Children are not scared of guns, they don't

fear shooting and even killing. When we were growing up, we would run if a soldier passed near your house with a gun, it was terrifying… but these children, it (gun) is like a toy.

In addition to uncontrolled availability of guns to the young people, children are involved in a number of activities that parents have no control over (Namuggala 2017). In the evening of a typical day for instance, children and youth move to the town center to watch Western movies and access social media sites. Such have exposed them to adult sexual content that traditionally was a taboo. Hence disregarding the secrecy and sacredness of sex to children.

Furthermore, as a result of the violence, displacement, and encampment, traditional emphasis on privacy, sacredness and timing related to sexuality has been lost. In the Western perspective, parents and state institutions have acknowledged and accepted adolescent sexual desire (Tolman 2002). In Africa, however, addressing sexuality is dependent on the concept of timing (Tamale 2011). Scholars have demonstrated that all through history Africans have discussed sexuality issues with their children (Mudhovozi et al. 2012) but at the right time, in the right setting, among the right people (Awopetu et al. 2013) and in gender-specific fora. From a cultural perspective, sexuality is a part of the socialization process, which is kept sacred and secret until the right time (marriage), which is determined by the community, especially the senior family members (Mudhovozi et al. 2012; Tamale 2011). But during and after the conflict, children have been abducted, defiled and raped. This has resulted in premarital pregnancies and births. Culturally, this means that children attain adulthood earlier than communally accepted.

While in the West the youth may be sexually active and still maintain their childhood status, in northern Uganda one is either sexually active or still a child. Given their experiences of war, many children have lost their innocence and thus socially acceptable childhood, which is attributed to innocence in form of sexual relations. Local communities, however, to some extent sustain conservative views about adolescent sexual engagement, with studies clearly elaborating that children's innocence is still valued and protected. This has resulted in communities blaming, stigmatizing, and hindering support to formerly abducted child mothers for example. Early pregnancies also provoke punishment since they bring shame to the family (see Awopetu et al. 2013). Parents thus marry off daughters who are suspected of engaging in sexual activity to avoid sociocultural embarrassment.

In northern Uganda, community responsibility for children has declined and in some cases been eroded. Despite the dynamic culture that Africa has adopted over the years, scholars have argued that some features have largely remained grounded. Swadener et al. (2000) note that among East African communities, "it takes a village to raise a child" where villages are contextually defined in forms of extended families, larger communities, and nations. The responsibility of raising a child is shouldered by everyone, including siblings, aunties, mothers, co-wives, and even grandparents (Boakye-Boaten 2010). Unlike Western constructions that label child fostering with grandmothers and other relatives child neglect, in Africa it is reflective of communal ties, identity and belonging (Christiansen et al. 2006). This has become more regularized with the rise of HIV/AIDS, which claims mainly the lives of the younger generation. Increased numbers have been recorded due to HIV/AIDS and war (Howard 2013).

Communal support networks are also impacted by generational variances. Adults who lived in settled communities prior to conflicts believe in communal responsibility for child upbringing. Children who lived in camps focus on individual survival. These different generational perceptions partly explain the rebellious tendencies of youths toward elders, especially when it comes to roles and responsibilities intended for sustenance of the community.

New questions that deconstruct the traditional understandings of the role of family and home likewise have emerged in post-conflict northern Uganda. The traditional cultural understanding of the family centers on parents, children and other relatives. In this study, however, participants explained that during the displacement children who were unaccompanied were no longer readily adopted as would be traditionally expected. Instead children who were not related by blood came together and formed new families. This created a new understanding of family based not on lineage or blood as culturally expected, but rather on friendship, challenges, and support for each other. Due to survival hardships, there was limited community commitment and willingness to adopt minors. Children themselves initiate, comprise, and support their own families out of necessity; hence the increasing child-headed household phenomena. Children therefore had to survive by themselves amidst limited access to communal resources especially land, limited adult guidance and insecurity.

Due to broken cultural and social networks, traditional roles of children and adults are changing too. Children are taking on familial roles and responsibilities, which challenge the position of elders as centers of indigenous knowledge whose experiences are critical for community knowledge production. The applicability of elders' knowledge becomes limited since it constructs childhood as fixed, meaning that the experiences of elders can sufficiently apply to all children in that community. Based on current research, childhood is a process, which is dynamic and varies according to the contexts and environment under which children are born and live. Children thus have experiences that prior to conflict were unheard of, for instance, abductions. For instance, "of the estimated 7500 girls abducted, 1000 conceived children while captive" (Mogwanja 2006: 2). If reconstruction programs are informed primarily by the lived experiences of elders, then, many will not comprehend the needs of formerly captured young mothers. It is thus important to understand how children seek to position themselves within broadly constructed frameworks. Although elders can help to create positive images within the memories of children, it is clear that their experiences are different and may not apply to the returned formerly displaced children. Reconstruction programming based on consultations with elders and their experiences may have limited applicability. Reconstruction blatantly demands active involvement of children and youth in issues that affect them.

I have discussed this far childhood in relation to adulthood. There is however, a transitional phase, youthhood that connects adulthood and childhood. The discussion on childhood cannot be complete without tackling youthhood. Participants explained the complexity of this stage while at the same time emphasizing how instrumental it is individually and communally. The next chapter explores the concept of youthhood in northern Uganda examining the intersectional nature of this stage of human development.

Conclusion

It is important that children embrace their rights, and use them for their protection, provision, and participation. Rights however, have to be conceptualized in contextually relevant ways that draw meaning to children's lived realities (Liebel 2012). This is because any attempt to universalize childhood (and youthhood) "leads only to a misunderstanding of the world of children, as well as interpretation fallacies" (Boakye-Boaten 2010: 105). Crucial also is linking children as rights holders with adults as duty bearers. This relationship can give attention to children's voices and participation in decision-making while holding adults accountable for actualization of such rights.

Childhood therefore needs to be conceptualized from 'below' to cater for children and childhoods on the margins. Childhood should be specific to social, cultural, economic, historical and political contexts in which children grow up, and the various meanings and implications these have on children. I concede with Afrocentric scholars over the need to challenge, unpack and deconstruct Western concepts and theories as a critical step for the liberation of African culture, beliefs, practices and childhoods (Chilisa 2012; Wane 2011).

Reconstructing childhood from an African perspective is one step toward decolonization and reclamation of African identity. Boakye-Boaten (2010) emphasizes "the continuous existence of any society depends on the ability of the society to socialize its children in the art of survival and cultural perpetuation" (104). It is this that childhood in Africa should target. The lives of children and young people in situations of conflict, therefore, need to become integral parts of peace agreements and peacebuilding processes. Above all, there is a need to increase the protection of children in armed conflict, ensure their education, their access to humanitarian assistance and to rehabilitation and reintegration. Communities in post-conflict northern Uganda are more complex both in composition and ideologies grounded in gender, age, and levels of education, marital and parental statuses. All these various dimensions need to be considered in the humanitarian assistance in order to provide a more holistic approach that reflects the experiences of these communities.

Given the preceding discussion, I acknowledge that numeric age is important for understanding human growth and development. It cannot, however, be used solely to determine childhood, youthhood, and adulthood especially in the developing world. I therefore emphasize that age is one other social variable just like gender, class, and ethnicity and should be used along with other identity markers relevant to particular communities to determinant childhood and adulthood.

References

Africa Renew. (2013, May). *Youth unemployment: Lessons from Ethiopia.* https://www.un.org/africarenewal/magazine/may-2013/youth-unemployment-lessons-ethiopia.

Awopetu, R. G., Ihuoma, I., & Newton, R. (2013). Attitude and perception of adolescents towards teenage pregnancy in Makurdi Metropolis. *Gender & Behaviour, 11*(1), 5272–5277.

Ayebe, S., Khan, S., & Sumberg, J. (2017). Africa's youth employment challenge: New perspectives. *IDS Bulletin: Transforming Development Knowledge, 48*(3), 1–12. Institute of Development Studies.

Bass, L. E. (2004). *Child labor in sub-Saharan Africa.* Boulder: Lynne Rienner.

Bird, K., & Higgins, K. (2009). *Conflict, education and the intergenerational transmission of poverty in northern Uganda.* London: Overseas Development Institute.

Boakye-Boaten, A. (2010). Changes in the concept of childhood: Implications on children in Ghana. *Journal of International Social Research, 3*(10), 104–115.

Bourdillon, M. (2006). Children and work: A review of current literature and debates. *Development and Change, 37*(6), 1201–1226.

Boyden, J., & de Berry, J. (Ed.). (2004). *Children and youth on the front line: Ethnography, armed conflict and displacement.* Studies in Forces Migration. New York and Oxford: Berghahn Books.

Cheney, K. (2007). *Pillars of the nation: Child citizens and Ugandan national development.* Chicago and London: The University of Chicago Press.

Cheney, K. (2010). Deconstructing childhood vulnerability: An introduction. *Childhood in Africa, 2*(1), 4–7. The Institute for the African Child, Ohio University.

Cheney, K. E. (2011). Children as ethnographers: The importance of participatory research in assessing orphans' needs. In *Childhood, 18*(2), 166–79.

Chilisa, B. (2012). *Indigenous research methodologies.* Thousand Oaks, CA: Sage.

Christiansen, C., Utas, M., & Vigh, H. E. (Eds.). (2006). *Navigating youth generating adulthood: Social becoming in an African context.* Uppsala: Nordiska Afrikaninstitute.

Dolan, C. (2009). *Social torture: The case of northern Uganda, 1986–2006.* New York and Oxford: Berghahn Books.

Goodmark, L. (2008). When is a battered woman not a battered woman? When she fights back. *Yale Journal of Law & Feminism, 20*(1), 75–129.

Howard, S. (Ed.). (2013). Childhood in Africa. *An Interdisciplinary Journal, 3*(1). 2009 ISSN 1948-6502.

Human Rights Watch. (2005). *Uprooted and forgotten: Impunity and human rights abuses in northern Uganda.* New York: Human Rights Organization.

Invernizzi, A. (2003). Street-working children and adolescents in Lima: Work as an agent of socialization. *Childhood, 10*(3), 319–341.

Kendall, N. (2010). Gendered moral dimensions of childhood vulnerability. *Childhood in Africa: An Interdisciplinary Journal, 1*(2), 26–37.

Khakshour, A., Abbasi, M. A., Sayedi, S. J., Saeidi, M., & Khodaee, G. H. (2015). *Child labor facts in the worldwide: A review article* (pp. 467–473). http://ijp.mums.ac.ir/article_3946_a1b99953d18ecf83e4229525a8200c9b.pdf.

Liebel, M. (2012). *Children's rights from below: Cross-cultural perspectives.* Basingstoke: Palgrave Macmillan.

Mogwanja, M. (2006). *Uganda donor update United Nations Children's Fund (UNICEF) Humanitarian Action.* Available at http://www.unicef.org/infobycountry/files/Uganda_final_DU_16May06.pdf.

Morrow, V. (2010). Should the world really be free of child labour? Some reflections. *Childhood, 17,* 435–440.

Morrow, V. (2011). *Understanding children and childhood* (Background Briefing Series No. 1). Lismore: Centre for Children and Young People, Southern Cross University.

Morrow, V. (2013). What's in a number? Unsettling the boundaries of age. *Childhood, 20,* 151–155. https://doi.org/10.1177/0907568213484199.

Mudhovozi, P., Ramarumo, M., & Sodi, T. (2012). Adolescent sexuality and culture: South African mothers' perspective. *African Sociological Review, 16*(2), 119–138.

Mutiibwa, P. (1992). *Uganda since independence: A story of unfulfilled hopes.* Trenton: Africa World Press.

Namuggala, V. F. (2015). Exploitation or empowerment? Adolescent female domestic workers in Uganda. *International Journal of Child, Youth and Family Studies, 6*(4), 561–580.

Namuggala, V. F. (2017). Gambling, dancing, sex work: Notions of youth employment in Uganda. In S. Ayebe, S. Khan, & J. Sumberg (Eds.), *Africa's youth employment challenge: New perspectives.* IDS Bulletin: Transforming Development Knowledge, 48 (3). Institute of Development Studies Press, University of Sussex.

Offit, T. (2008). *Conquistadores de la calle: Child street labor in Guatemala City.* Austin: University of Texas Press.

Panter-Brick, C., & Smith, T. M. (Eds.). (2004). *Abandoned children* (pp. 1–26). Cambridge: Cambridge University Press.

Sommers, M. (2006). *Fearing Africa's young men—The case of Rwanda* (Social Development Papers: Conflict Prevention and Reconstruction. No. 32).

Spitzer, H., & Twikirize, J. (2013). War affected children in northern Uganda: No easy path to normality. *International Social Work, 56,* 67–79.

Swadener, B. B., Kabiru, M., & Njenga, A. (2000). *Does the village still raise the child? A collaborative study of changing child-rearing and early education in Kenya.* Albany: State University of New York Press.

Tamale, S. (Ed.). (2011). *African sexualities: A reader.* Capetown: Pambazuka Press.

Temmerman, E. (2001). *Aboke girls: Children abducted in northern Uganda*. Kampala: Fountain Publishers.
Tolman, D. (2002). *Dilemmas of desire: Teenage girls talk about sexuality*. London: Havard University Press.
Tornberg, H. (2012). Ethnic fragmentation and political instability in post-colonial Uganda: Understanding the Contribution of Colonial Rule to the Plights of the Acholi People in northern Uganda. Human Rights Studies Fall 2012.
UNICEF. (2005). *Childhood under threat. The state of the world's children 2005*. https://www.unicef.org/sowc05/english/childhooddefined.html.
UNICEF. (2014). A survey on re-entry of pregnant girls in primary and secondary schools in Uganda. *Published on UNESCO HIV and Health Education Clearing house*. https://hivhealthclearinghouse.unesco.org.
Urdal, H. (2004). *The devil in the demographics: The effect of youth bulges on domestic armed conflict, 1950–2000* (Social Development Papers, Conflict Prevention and Reconstruction, No. 14).
Wane, N. (2011). African indigenous feminist thought. In N. Wane, A. Kempf, & M. Simmons (Eds.), *The politics of cultural knowledge* (pp. 7–21). New York: Springer.
War Child. (2015). The reality of child-headed households: Northern Uganda study. A longitudinal study on the affect of income generating activity on education and protection outcomes for children and child headed households in northern Uganda, June 16, 2015.
Wessels, M. (2006). *Child soldiers: From violence to protection*. Cambridge and London: Harvard University Press.

CHAPTER 5

We Are What We Are Not

> I would say a youth is not an adult. Neither are they children. They are not independent yet not entirely dependent on any one. They hate getting instructions yet they don't know what to do. Their definition is vague... Key Informant.

INTRODUCTION

In this chapter, I expound on the intersectional nature of the social category of the youth. The youth tend to belong to various categories simultaneously, which consequently places them nowhere in particular hence lacking belonging. Because the youth are "everywhere", local community uses dominant categorization of children and adults to explain what the youth are. What falls outside these two dominant categories describes generally who the youth are. This is because the youth cannot entirely identify with any of the socially standardized categories with which they (youth) relate. For instance they are neither children nor adults yet they significantly contribute to both categories and have characteristic attributes of each category. This chapter pays special attention to the complex subcategory of the female youth given their explicit exclusionary multidimensional identities. In examining gender-and age-related nuances, the chapter also brings out aspects relating to social justice and equality. The chapter in these aspects examines how youthhood plays out in access to and use of humanitarian assistance and other important post-conflict

© The Author(s) 2018
V. F. Namuggala, *Childhood, Youth Identity, and Violence in Formerly Displaced Communities in Uganda*, Critical Cultural Studies of Childhood, https://doi.org/10.1007/978-3-319-96628-1_5

reconstruction resources including land. I specifically explicate the cultural relevance of the concept of youth as gendered, choice, an economic concept as well as an educational and Western concept drawing on the lived realities of the formerly displaced young people in north eastern Uganda.

Like the chapter opening quote explains, the social understanding of the category of youth is simultaneously characterized by both vulnerabilities and potential. Youth are, for instance, actively involved in adult activities (locally associated with informed decision-making) although they cannot make independent decisions largely due to limited experience. The youth are thus expected to work under adult supervision, guidance, and mentoring. Unguided youth decisions account for the generational disagreements since they in most cases contradict elders' expectations. As I explore these dynamics, it is also crucial to assess how the youth maneuver and navigate through these social controls and related vulnerable situations. This chapter thus examines youth agency and capabilities amidst challenging socially policed survival situations.

I argue that single categorical constructions and analysis is limiting in understanding the experiences of youth who simultaneously occupy multiple categories. Teenage/child/young mothers, for instance, cannot fully pass as adults if they are not married. They can neither fit in the children's category because they have children. From a gendered perspective, the social understanding of youth is locally constructed to refer to young men. Female youth in such cases belong *everywhere* yet they in actual sense belong *nowhere* hence missing out on assistance and relief services, which target concretized specified categories. Local communities find concepts like "child mothers" as belittling and constraining female youth full identity as "real" mothers. The local community explains that one cannot be both a mother and a child as the child mother notion seems to suggest. Rather one can be either a mother or a child and not both. This, however, depends on the circumstances under which one finds herself. While such young mothers deserve special attention, as humanitarian agencies run programs targeting them, it is culturally limited. Such externally constructed identity markers unintentionally exclude some young women through self-exclusion. The young women have to decide whether to give up on communal belonging (by choosing not to fully embrace motherhood) but since status and belonging are crucial for social security, the majority choose to give up the externally awarded title of child mothers hence giving up on assistance. This highlights the issue of language in contextualizing experience as an important aspect. It is therefore important to use culturally appropriate language to bring out the lived realities in such communities.

There are discrepancies even in institutionalized dominant understandings of the concept of youth. Uganda defines youth to be individuals between 18 and 35 (Uganda National Youth Policy 2001). The UN, on the other hand, considers those between 15 and 24 years of age. What Uganda terms youth according to the international standards are adults. The definition of child, however, is anyone below the age of 18. What UN defines as youth are in some instance children if they are below 18 years. Youthhood, therefore, draws from both children and adults.

Cultural Relevance of the Concept Youth

In this section, I discuss the understanding of youthhood in the post-conflict phase. I however, wish to highlight that the stages of conflict, i.e. pre, during and post-stages are more fluid than fixed especially from a feminist understanding and no clear demarcations can be made between and among these stages. Some features for instance violence run through all the stages although with varying levels of intensity. The chapter thus only emphasizes the post-conflict state but similar arguments can still be made in pre-conflict and active conflict stages of violent conflict. Also, at some points the discussion draws on these stages of conflict for more clarity.

In northern Uganda, the differentiation between a child and adult seems to be clear though in various ways different from the Western understanding as earlier discussed. However, the differences between a child and a youth, and a youth and an adult are blurred. This is because many of the characteristics youth have are used in descriptions of both childhood and adulthood. Youthhood is the intermediate stage where individuals have specific features implicating all the three critical stages of human growth and development. As such a youth can bear both childhood and adulthood identifiers simultaneously. Study participants, for example, described themselves in complex ways depicting more than one category including "adult youth", "young adult", "grown child". Even though the adolescents have certain development competencies that distinguish them from the children, they, at the same time lack the social, cultural, and personal attributes that define adulthood (Morrow 2013).

They are thus out of the protected category of children yet they are vulnerable since they are not independent from the adult control, provision, and guidance. To bring out this simultaneity, one respondent after failing to come up with a definite description of a youth explained that,

> A youth is someone who has not had a child, yet they are not small children and can take care of themselves. Okay, in other words, youth are grown up children.

Taking care of themselves, in this case, does not allude to independence in economic terms or decision-making. It refers to individual/personal aspects like bathing yourself, washing one's clothes and generally minimizing the burden of reproductive and domestic responsibilities rendered to that person by the immediate caregiver. Youth, therefore, take care of themselves but within the limits provided by the adults under whose jurisdiction they reside. Youthhood is thus a transformational phase, which transitions one into adulthood following fulfillment of social expectations. In addition, youthhood is a highly gendered construction. A female key informant, working with a local NGO explained:

> Culturally when a girl reaches around the age of 12 years, but especially after her first menses, a rope is tied around the ankle of the right leg to signify that she can be booked and this shows that she is approaching maturity. This girl is being trained to change from childhood to adulthood... The boy on the other hand is given land to build a house and prepare to marry and start his family.

Until the booking is done or the house has been built for girls and boys, respectively, these are still referred to as children, i.e. a girl and a boy. This, however, automatically switches to adulthood when requirements are met. The concept of youth is thus not culturally grounded although it is increasingly gaining significance with the implementation of humanitarian assistance, particularly in the post-conflict stage. While childhood and youthhood are generally described in related terms, there were some specific explanations focused on the youth that were not really applicable to the understanding of a child. Besides humanitarian assistance programs' description of youth (male and female) in a uniform way, which is drawn from the dominant frameworks, the informal local setting provides other forms of categorization, which inform their understanding of a youth. It is on these local perspectives that this section focuses.

Culturally in Soroti, youthhood was described as a time in passing from childhood to adulthood, which relied heavily on the body's ability and readiness to perform adult functions. Young people are termed youth when able to procreate and adults when they actualize the anticipated ability by procreating. Like childhood, youthhood is also applied differently for boys and girls. Gender also leads to differentiated impacts for both boys and girls. For instance, marriage and procreation were critical for women, while protection and provision mattered most for the men. Youthhood could thus be termed the "potentiality stage" while adulthood is the "actualization stage". If one's potential is not demonstrated, then that person's status and identity does not elevate to adulthood. What the participants described as a youth from a gendered perspective was:

> …for girls when menstruation sets in, that girl is ready for marriage and is considered able to have children… whether she has her first menses at 11 years, it demonstrates her potential to be a mother someday. Menstruation shows that the body is grown and ready…The boy is able to put up a grass-thatched house, ready to bring in a wife. The house shows ability to head and protect a family. The house should not leak or grass be blown off by wind. It has to be built with utmost care.

While biological considerations are appreciated, these are accomplished by social constructions through performativity and functionality. Describing a female youth as someone who is ready for marriage or who can have children is potentiality. This description concurrently draws on both biological determinism (menstruation) as well as sociocultural narratives. Women, in this case, continue to be valued mainly for reproduction of the community while the men are charged with its development and security. This could explain why humanitarian programing especially for the youth was locally perceived as male youth oriented since recovery aid was meant for development purposes.

Definitions of youthhood are embedded in constructions of power, authority, and social worth (Christiansen et al. 2006). Adolescent girls specifically are faced with more vulnerabilities at this stage of their development at individual, familial, and societal levels. Girls for instance face higher rates of early marriages, limited access to family planning services, higher rates of HIV infection, and high dropout rates from formal schools. Frameworks that emphasize the rights of the child tend to marginalize young adults. The youth therefore minimally benefit from reconstruction programming. It is thus crucial to emphasize that if youth are to benefit, frameworks and policy approaches need to recognize contextual differences as well as outstanding forms of marginalization in such contexts where youth experiences are embedded. This is important because social policies that fail to promote equality may result in subordination, marginalization, and exclusion of certain portions of the population (Kabeer 2008).

The previous quote also clarifies the role of elders in the lives of the youth. While they are permitted to build their houses, these are done in proximity to their parents for continued guidance and direction. This also means access to family land and other resources are reliant in respect of elders and promotion of family ties. This also provides social security for instance in cases of aged parents. This is because the youth are considered energetic and can do any work yet at the same time, they have less in terms of property ownership, access, and control. They almost entirely depends on their parents for survival. Conceptualization of youth in this area thus demands a focus on not only age but also the generational power hierarchies, which inform relations, and networks that youth forge. It would also require examination of institutional frameworks through which the youth forge their agency and resilience, and the same frameworks through which their voices are silenced.

It is locally acknowledged that decisions affecting life are based on the lived experience. What the youth lack, therefore, is the lived experience to make informed decisions for their individual benefit as well as benefit and safety of the communities to which they belong. When these are attained and demonstrated then adulthood is achieved, which means involvement in public decision-making and leadership. One female key informant explained the importance of marriage in Teso culture:

> If you are not married, you have no right to speak in public. Even when you are toothless (elderly) but without a family, you cannot say anything sensible, no one listens to you, no one believes in your capabilities. If you cannot run a family, what can you do? How can you guide the community?

The family is the smallest basic yet central unit of society. In this unit skills attributed to leadership are trained, attained, and demonstrated publically. One's ability to sustain a family, therefore, demonstrates their potential for communal leadership. In the family, skills for resolving conflict, planning, and general leadership are taught and learnt. Young people especially males, however, due to the economic breakdown tend to stay longer in youthhood since they cannot pay bride price to attain a socially acceptable marriage, which affects their active participation in communal activities (see Sommers 2007). Just like childhood, there is a very narrow distinction between a youth and an adult. For instance, when a female conceives, she is no longer a potential parent but a "real" parent hence an adult through that performativity. This can be evidenced from the explanation below given by a 26-year-old female respondent.

> I am a youth as well as an adult. I am still in the age category of a youth. I say I am an adult because I am above 18 and I have children. What would you call me? Adult youth? I also have other dependents that I care and provide for. I am therefore an adult. But to tell you the truth in the community I am an adult and I like it.

The above participant understands the formal understanding of a youth according to the Ugandan constitution as someone between the ages of 18 and 35. She combines this formal definition with the local adult understanding as someone with children. These positions her simultaneously as both yet humanitarian programming largely considers single categorical identifications. Humanitarian agencies, therefore, compel individuals to choose either category in order to benefit from the aid provided. Such a choice is however, not an individual one since such individuals work in relation to the entire community. Choosing one category could as well comprise such individual's positionality socially. Individuals thus have to adopt a description, which is communally acceptable. Coming up with a new concept "adult youth" explains how complex categorization can be, as well as the limitations such categories have. Distributing aid through rigid categories like household heads, children, and youth hinders access and use by some of the most marginalized community members. Individuals who simultaneously occupy more than one category for instance "adult youth" as reflected above may not fall in either of the categories, i.e. youth or adults, which hinders their resettlement.

Education, Choice, and Identity

Besides performativity, in northern eastern Uganda, youthhood is also understood in various ways including through formal education and also as a choice individuals can make. Attending school provides an important feature for understanding youth in northern Uganda as an educational concept especially for the humanitarian programs. Youth are thus categorized in two major categories, i.e. "out-of-school" and "in-school" youth. The programs are therefore implemented in appreciation of the fact that some youth are in, while others are out of school. While their age is considered, specific programs are run for these educationally different youth groups. This is based on the fact that out-of school youth have a lot of "free" time on them so they are more involved. Prior to this categorization, youth-in schools had to choose between school and attending youth development programs, since these programs were run during school hours. Given the immediate benefits provided by the reconstruction programs juxtaposed against constrained survival mechanisms, youth were prioritizing immediate survival needs over schooling. Thus, programs were delivered considering the heterogeneous nature of the youth. This is, however, not the case for the local community. The communal perceptions do not consider those out of school as youth especially if they are married or have children. Irrespective of their age, locally, these out-of-school youth are considered adults. Schooling is thus one activity that prolongs youthhood since it halts performance of adult roles for instance childbirth and marriage. While some of the young people with children would return to school, it is not a common trend.

The young people who are out of school but not married are considered to be in transition and have increased access to resources including land to enhance their transformation. This transition stage is, however, tricky especially when one stays in it for a long time. This led to what some local community members termed as a new construction grounded on individual choice. In this construction, individuals decide what they want to be within the community by not complying with the predetermined communal standards.

Youthhood as a choice: Since youthhood is not recognized culturally as a stage of development, some community members termed it to be a personal choice individuals could make. To these people, youthhood is not a category among the population groups but rather an entirely individual choice. This choice could be made by refuting/challenging/ or not meeting the socially recognized and respected terms of adulthood especially childbirth and marriage. This choice is reflected in young people who have the capacity to relate and function like adults but do not actualize it practically. To emphasize this understanding, one participant explains,

> Someone who does not stay with a man (or woman) i.e. not married or cohabiting with a man, although they have all the features for that, are the youth. They have no reason not to be married but just decide to be single in order to enjoy life; they do not want to work as married women do.

What this means is that one can choose to be a youth all their life. This choice comes with freedom especially from male control. Such women can move to wherever they wish and conduct themselves as they please. The choice to be single is a transformative venture since it challenges generalized local narratives that marriage is the ultimate goal for every woman. Despite communal pressure and policing put on young adults, staying single by choice demonstrates that there are women who enjoy being single or sexually active without being married and/or having children. This is transformative as womanhood can be fronted in its own self without reference to wifehood or motherhood. However, like in many other choices individuals make, this comes at a cost especially from the community. Grown-ups who do not want to have children are called youth because they fear responsibility, which connotes maturity. Because, they do not demonstrate their capability to the society, they are undervalued and under looked, as they are believed to front selfish interests over communal ones.

In direct contrast to choice is the group of people who are constrained in meeting socially expected adulthood attributes. The general community for instance generally sympathizes with young women who cannot have biological children since they are considered to be miserable and vulnerable. To achieve public sympathy, however, requires one to demonstrate that they have tried all they can in vain. For instance, someone can be married for a long time without conceiving, seeks advice from other women and elders with no much success. It thus takes a public declaration of one's biological incapability (infertility) to attain social sympathy. Despite receiving less judgment and prejudice socially, such people rarely get to participate as leaders since they are believed to lack the experiences families provide for public leadership.

Besides lived experience-based explanations, some informants also explained youthhood as being a foreign construct. In their description of a youth, they highlighted it to be culturally ungrounded but a Western way of trying to understand the Africans. In one of the FGDs they described a youth as,

> ...someone who likes to wear Western fashions (clothes) like jeans, necklaces and chains (jewelry for both male and female), and mini- skirts. They adopt the Western culture and way of life including dressing, eating, walking and talking. They go to nightclubs frequently. They hate local food and enjoy chips and chicken (fast food) and speak with swag especially in English-yeah man!... male youth plait hair in lines too. When you see that, then you know that person is a youth.

The people who live this kind of life are locally identified as the youth. The local description of the youth is highly reflective of the young men. While such understanding is labeled Western, it is not as derogatory as when used in reference to young women. Young women who conduct themselves in a "modern way" are negatively described as loose, and spoilt. In addition to the impact of the war as a factor contributing to early sexual encounters, some participants also suggested that sexual activeness among youth could also be explained by this Western imported culture since youth (male and female) tend to interact a lot with limited adult supervision. There is thus a culture that has been socially understood to identify the youth. This "youth culture" is positioned as outlaying and incompatible with the pre-conflict sociocultural orientation. The study of such culture demands shifting away from studying youth as a stage of human development to studying youth in its own right (Christiansen et al. 2006). Youth are in this way conceptualized as agentic and able to situate within or detach themselves from local and global trends.

While there are exceptions, youthhood is generally perceived with negative connotations. The youth were described for instance as drunkards with no morals. The youth raised in the camp also lack respect for elders and thus rarely seek elders' guidance and counsel. As such, youth do not think about the future and constantly make wrong decisions. While previous scholars noted that youth especially the male drink out of frustration (Dolan 2009), in this study we discovered that this wasn't entirely true. Responses pointed to the fact that youth drink as a demonstration of status, i.e. economic and personal independence. Drinking was one-way youth renegotiated their social realm through taking respect, forging identity and belonging amongst themselves. Youthhood is thus intertwined with notions of power, and belonging in highly gendered ways. One participant elaborated:

> …as a way of showing off money and "modernity", the youth take a lot of alcohol, cigarettes and opium (weed/marijuana) publically… It is also a way of demonstrating their maturity especially among other youth. They also do it to prove that they are now independent and no longer children controlled and guided over their lives.

Despite such conduct, it was noted that youth constantly deny all responsibility of their situation and always blame other persons for their position. This is another marker of lack of maturity since adults are expected to be responsible for their actions. One key informant dreaded the continued lack of self-responsibility by youth noting that they lead reckless lives and then blame parents and authority for failing to protect them. This description links back to the protection narratives as well as the rights informed understanding of childhood discussed earlier in the previous chapters. Youth, due to sensitization largely by children's rights organizations argue that both their parents and the state failed to protect them and thus should be held responsible for their current situation. The youth thus evoke childhood experiences to explain their current circumstances.

Some theories explaining situations of violent situations involving youth allude to idleness and irresponsibility of the youth—the youth bulge theory (Urdal 2006), some community members in agreement observed that youth were not willing and at times unable to participate in activities like agriculture and other economically productive ventures due to lack of both skills and resources especially land. Because the youth need money especially for drinking, they are involved in petty crimes like stealing and selling of animals, and other personal items like phones, which they acquire through, pickpocketing. A big number of youth are also involved in gambling activities for instance in sports betting in order to earn "quick and easy" cash (Namuggala 2017). Instead of working in the gardens, it is more rewarding and easy to keep in the town center and play such games. But when they lose, they resort to stealing and robbing others. Youth are also involved in dubious activities like gun theft, alcoholism, and drug abuse. In some cases, their frustration also leads to intimate partner violence, all of which affects development and reconstruction programming.

The youth are also easily caught up in violent eruptions—even those that do not concern them directly. Participants mentioned that disgruntled youth call upon others and organize attacks on other people (gang fights). One briefly explained that; "you may find about ten male youth attacking a family in which one family member disagreed with one group member. They attack in weird hours of the night". Such features conform to dominant theories relating to youth as a security threat. The study findings indicate that youth are generally violent. I, however, disagree with other scholars that gender and age cause violence (Mesquida and Wiener 1999; Urdal 2006). I argue that due to the long marginalization youth in conflict situations have encountered, violence has been normalized in their lives hence conceive it as the most viable conflict resolution mechanism. Also, communities expect youth to survive and demonstrate their progression towards adulthood, to which economic empowerment is a critical component. The failure of the youth to meet community expectations also results in frustration and self-doubt for the youth. Therefore, the energy they would put in productive work is invested in the criminal activity. The following section elaborates more on youth involvement in violence.

YOUTHHOOD AS A CONTRIBUTOR TO VIOLENCE

Youthhood in itself is a complex concept. It even gets more complicated when one tries to understand it from the perspective of violence. While all developing countries' population rates are increasing, Africa is unique because of the overwhelming young population. With the exception of a few countries in Southern Africa and some island nations, the World Bank, in its 2015 report, notes, "fertility rates and youth dependency rates in sub-Saharan Africa are among the highest in the world, exposing the region to higher poverty rates, smaller investments in children, lower labor productivity, high unemployment or underemployment, and the risk of political instability" (1). Without economic opportunity and marginalization from politics, violence emerges as a rational and, seemingly, the most effective means for youth to make demands and engage the system. Youth in formerly displaced communities present a unique conceptualization of (un)employment, which problematizes formal constructions relating to employment. It was noted for instance that youth are not necessarily unemployed and idle as dominant frameworks assert but rather are involved in income generating activities, which are socially and morally undermined, some of these are also illegal and thus not considered work. Youth are involved in sports betting, prostitution, and contemporary dancing as forms of work (Namuggala 2017).

The theoretical conceptualization of the youth as a threat was coined by a number of Western-based contributors including Gaston Bouthou, Jack A, Goldstone, Gary Fuller, and Gunnar Heinsohn. The youth bulge theory (YBT) examines the likelihood of a conflict based on the logic that a large proportion of young men in the population will make a country more vulnerable to instability. Mesquida and Wiener argue (1999), "the most reliable factor in explaining episodes of coalitional aggression is the relative abundance of young males" (181). Scholars have also recently asserted that youth create susceptibility to violence more than religious fundamentalism (Urdal 2011), which was considered a leading cause of violence following the September 11, 2001 attacks (Rogers et al. 2007). Mesquida and Wiener (1999) specifically argue that people who go out and kill other people are males aged between 16 and 30 years. Youth demographics are thus a big threat to global security from the perspective of the international community.

The theory emphasizes that "young men are more prone to violence than either older men or women" (Sommers 2007: 103). Such conceptualization pathologizes young men. In addition to using chronological age to apportion responsibility and blame for violence, the YBT has a gender-biased construction portraying young women as entirely submissive and passive. This victimizing portrayal disadvantages young women in post conflict reconstruction. In situations of peacebuilding for instance, limited attention is paid to female youth concerns since they are not expected to amount into instability. YBT has therefore been used to support policy directions that are unhelpful to development, peace, and youth (Sommers 2007). Stereotypes relating to emotions are further emphasized in this YB theory where young men can be angry and demonstrate such anger publically, while young women are not expected to. It is therefore important to understand how the use of age, gender, class, and location in defining and theorizing youth can/has affect(ed) youth identity formation in Uganda.

This section juxtaposes the findings from northeastern Uganda with conventional theorizing relating to violence. Specifically, it focuses on the youth bulge theory, which constructs poor young men as violent (Urdal 2006). I assert that youth in the Third World (Global South and poor north) have been misrepresented by mainstream conventional Western conceptualization as a security threat. I argue with other scholars that several historical, societal, and political tensions influence one another to facilitate violence and conflict in the developing world (Kasozi 2013). This also applies among poor people (Brainard and Chollet 2007), people of color (Crenshaw 2012) and indigenous communities in the developed world (Smith 2006). I conclude that the huge numbers of poor male youth in Uganda cannot therefore solely explain violence as the YBT suggests. It is also true that what the YBT constructs as youth, are in most cases locally perceived as adults. For the local communities, therefore, it is not the youth but rather adults in the community who participate in violence. Performativity, therefore, determines who one is and not their numeric age.

In order to explore further the gendered nature of youthhood earlier explained, this chapter also incorporates feminist approaches to violence and conflict. I use feminist epistemologies to facilitate an alternative understanding of youth identity (re)construction, prioritizing gender as a category of analysis. Gender is here presented as intersectional, bearing direct relation to numeric age, location, and biological development to inform identity constructions and belonging. All this is based on the lived experiences of the communities involved in this study. While dominant views are important, I prioritize local voices while examining causes and experiences of armed conflict. Understanding violence from the standpoint of the youth minimizes imperialistic, racial, gender and class marginalization involved in Western conventional theories such as the YBT.

Feminist Critiques to the Youth Bulge Theory

In this discussion, I accord emphasis to feminist epistemologies grounded in theorizing from lived experience, deconstructing dominant discourse (in this case Western and patriarchal), false universalization and essentialism. I thus call for community involvement and privileging community-based understanding of the causes of violence.

Youth are members of communities and act in relation to other community members. Shepherd (2008) and Butler (2010) have both argued that violence is relational and intersectional. This challenges YBT's use of socially constructed stereotypes to draw biologically unproven conclusions (Sommers 2011). It is thus important to understand men not only as individuals but also as members of a collective community that relate with others including women, mothers and children. Violence is thus a communal venture to which all community members contribute. When responding to youth involvement in violence, one male youth probably in his late teens said,

> Youth are the majority in situations of violence but everyone is part of it including women, men, and even children. Even elders in most cases give instructions especially in case of group attacks, encourage the youth and even bless them to go for such fights. They don't fight physically but emotionally. They evoke the spirit world and this is very crucial for the youth to know that the spirits are okay with what is going on.

Feminists use relationality to elaborate a critical feature of war noting that individual freedom of action is defined and limited by social relationships (Alcoff 2006; Butler 2010). Individual decisions are "never completely limited and never without any limits" (Sjoberg 2013: 180). As such you cannot explain armed violence relying solely on young men without understating how they relate to other members in the society. Alcoff (2006) notes, "the individual is a construct mediated by social discourses beyond individual control or intervention" (140) since individuals exist in relation to others Oyewumi (1997). What this implies is that addressing violence should not target specific individuals but rather systems, processes, and structures through which such individuals operate. This is a critical observation and has practical implications. Handling war crimes for instance as individual cases has been problematic for northern Uganda. The ICC, for instance, issued arrest warrants for Joseph Kony failing to appreciate similarities between the rebel group and the government groups in violation of human rights (Branch 2007).

Looking at the physical fighting and violence is one big limitation of the youth bulge theory. Physical attacks are just a demonstration of frustrations in the community. Roles relating to violence are divided basing on the position in society and age. The energetic portion of the population gets involved in the energetic phase. Focusing only on youth therefore fails to understand the organization in the community. In addition, the youth bulge theory is also limited in concentrating on male youth only in the public sphere. This disregards in the private aspects of society yet they continually influence the public. It is therefore difficult to understand the public place in isolation from the private. It can be argued that the theory's neglect of private spaces accounts for its neglect of the role of female youth and elders in the case of northern Uganda.

Hendrixson (2004) argues against the theory's biological construction of violence. The theory, she argues (to which I also agree) creates differentiated biological threats for boys and girls resulting in "a dual threat of explosive violence and explosive fertility" (1), respectively. The boys are extremely violent while the girls are extremely fertile thereby increasing the population densities significantly. Hendrixson notes further that the theory "reflects and is reflected in racial, gender and age discrimination" (1) and the use of the "power of numbers envisages racial, cultural and gender stereotypes" (4). The youth bulge theory implies that young men with constricted options will automatically and necessarily respond with violent rebellion, which may not always be the case. This assumes voluntary participation of the youth yet in situations like northern Uganda, children and youth were abducted and forcefully recruited into armed forces. One former soldier in his early 20s said,

> If we could choose, I would never have fought but we were grabbed from our house in the night and taken by the rebels. You have no choice but to fight. It is a matter of life and death. When you are attacked, you either kill them or they kill you. At times we heard some children were taken by the Ugandan army, and returned back home but you never know what your fate is.

Sommers (2007), on the other hand challenges the theory from an African grounded perspective. He emphasizes YBT's failure to explain why African cities, the centers of the youth concentrations especially due to rural–urban migration are not centers for major violent conflicts. Sub-Saharan Africa's wars such as the LRA in northern Uganda and Sudanese Peoples Liberation Army (SPLA) have largely been rural based battle-fields (Sommers 2006).

Butler (2010) carries on this further noting that wars are normally fought among "ungrievable lives"—those are lives that cannot be lost, cannot be destroyed, because they already inhabit a lost and destroyed zone. It is thus not about numbers but where the people that have no life live that wars are staged. In the context of Uganda, the northern part is this zone. Such zones are ontologically already lost and destroyed which means when they are destroyed in war, nothing is destroyed (ibid.). This is a valid description of how the developed world treats lives in the developing world. For instance, the United States justified violence against 'barbaric' countries including Iraq, and Afghanistan to maintain security internally. Uganda's central government justified war in the northern region to maintain security and peace in the south.

In addition, Sommers (2007) applies a postcolonial approach to elaborate that what youth are blamed for today was a historical creation. In Africa the situation was generally a creation of colonialism. Using the case of Nairobi, Sommers (2007) further notes that the city has an "overwhelmingly urban population in part because British colonialists recruited men to work in Nairobi while prohibiting them from bringing their families along" (105). Increasing male youth urban population is thus a way of attaining the masculine attributes constructed by the colonizers, i.e. earning wage payment.

The solutions the YBT provides also have limited applicability to Africa. While it is very important for development, study findings provide reasons to doubt the ability of education to provide a durable solution for violence as the YBT argues. Like in many other children and youth concerns (including child labor, prostitution, HIV/AIDS) education has not provided a practical solution, which is indicative of the limited impact education accords youth economic empowerment. If unemployment was the problem, then job creation rather than education would be the solution. Emphasizing formal education, therefore, becomes a Western-imposed approach that does not reflect local livelihood demands. Respondents from northern Uganda emphasized the need for practical skills as a way of reintegrating the youth. For this study, the theory provided a starting point for understanding why post-conflict programs and processes in Uganda have focused on male youth, as well as demobilization and disarmament other than social reintegration. The sole application of the YBT, however, lacks the explanatory power to understand how female and male youth reintegrate in post-conflict settings, especially better understanding of their agency and resilience. It is also insufficient in explaining how the youth rebuild their lives in the post-conflict situations. While discussing the civil war in northern Uganda and the impact it has had on girls, Boyden and

Berry (2004) argue that the investigation of victimization requires a critical examination of the specific ways in which people are made and become vulnerable in the context in which they live. This calls for understanding systems, process, and structures that have informed the situation in northern Uganda rather than blaming particular portions of the community.

I argue the solutions to solve the conflict problem must be rooted within the community and the best way this can be done is through active local youth and community participation. In trying to come up with suggestions targeting long-term peace building, some respondents believed in collective responsibility for the sustenance of the northern Uganda war. One leader said,

> No one can be blamed for violence. We are all part of it and we all participate but in different ways, some of which are less obvious. Children, youth, elders, women, men, even community and religious leaders. We all have contributed in some way. When pointing at those that are publically known as former fighters, we just need to find someone to blame for what went wrong. Of course our levels of involvement are different but we all did something. If we can stop pointing fingers, we would rebuild ourselves.

This means blaming is not going to provide any progressive peace in the region. It is important to shift beyond the labeling of specific categories to examine the causes of violence and thus dully deal with them in the search for sustainable peace and development. To this, feminists move beyond critiquing the youth bulge theory, and provide an alternative way to positively understand violence. Feminist scholars have thus theorized emotions and specifically anger. In the next section, I briefly examine how "felt" theory (Million 2009) explains and justifies the anger particular communities might have and display.

Labeling youth of color as "angry young men" is imperialistic and racist and deserves deconstruction since it hinders non-Western knowledge production, intentionally to patronize and dominate the third world thereby maintaining power hierarchies. I agree with Jaggar (2008) that emotions (in this case anger) are socially and historically created and thus stretch beyond nature or biological explanations. Theories based on the biology therefore demand a deconstruction in favor of those based on the social experiences of communities involved. Theorizing should therefore be done from the perspective of the most marginalized to cater for the multiple forms of relegations such individuals endure.

Importantly, the feminist approach recommends looking at violence and conflict as sensed. This highlights the felt element of wars (Butler 2010; Sjoberg 2013, 2014), which have been totally disregarded by conventional theories of violence including development and human rights perspectives. I contend defining war would take on new dimensions if it were understood as a lived experienced. It recognizes that youth have physical bodies, feelings, and experiences of violence which need to be understood if peace is to be attained. Conceptualizing war as sensed thus brings on new questions, perspectives and knowledge to transform studies on violence. Previously pathologized forms of knowledge including emotions like anger become validated. Validation of such knowledge breaks silences and gatekeepers in institutions including academia, religion, and research (Million 2009).

Sjoberg (2013) emphasizes that knowledge cannot be separated from its relationship with the knower which makes it context-dependent, subjective, and political simultaneously. It is thus a glaring oversight for traditional theories to claim representation of everyone by speaking to the dominant class members, in this case being the adults. Like standpoint feminists have elaborated, the multiply marginalized provide a more complex and objective view of reality (Collins 2000; Harding 1993) and attending to their concerns, automatically cater for other members who may be singly or doubly marginalized (Crenshaw 1989).

In summation, I wish to emphasize that while gender has been integrated in theorizing violence, it still remains peripheral and has not become a central part of research programs outside feminist security studies (Sjoberg 2014). Conflict should be understood as a system that has tools, agents, structures all of which are interconnected (Sjoberg 2013). While it disadvantages the marginalized, those with power benefit from it, which makes it hard to solve. Connecting the various forms and levels of violence would facilitate understanding outstanding questions like; why conflict results in more women as refugees and the ways in which poverty makes women more vulnerable in natural disasters. Traditional theorizing has looked at war as an event with a specified beginning and end well defined and clearly demarcated. However, "rather than being an event, war is a continuum, a practice and a symbolic politics or performance" (Sjoberg 2013: 39). Critical feminists argue that women are always at war in their families and communities and at times with their bodies yet patriarchal violence is systemic and women at times contribute to such violence. It is thus vital to rethink security and violence as "made and made in gendered ways" (Wibben 2011: 106).

War is not event that is just caused and practiced or performed but also sensed and experienced. Understanding war as sensed and experienced changes not only how it is to be evaluated but rather how it is to be defined and understood (Sjoberg 2013: 277). For instance violence against women and girls only changes in intensity, form and frequency but is evident in what is formally termed pre-conflict and post-conflict phases of armed violence. Wartime rape, forced marriages, and pregnancies are some experiences to show that war physically and emotionally affects bodies and thus indeed an experience. Conceptualizing youth experience demands exploration of their experiences during and after conflict. It is thus crucial to involve youth in post-conflict reconstruction if their concerns are to be addressed.

Youth involvement indicates appreciation of their agency. The importance of human agency lies at the heart of a paradigm that recognizes the role of social actors (Moser and Clark 2001). The experience of violent conflict therefore with social life is and cannot be built upon a single discourse (in this case gender or age). "Individual women (and youth) as social actors improvise alternative ways of formulating life objectives, despite the restrictive resources, social relations and environment" (ibid.: 5). According to Alcoff (2006: 140), "the individual is a construct mediated by social discourses beyond individual control or intervention" Theories of conflict thus need to refrain from presenting young people especially the women as a totally victimized and vulnerable group. Important to acknowledge is that displaced women and girls have resilience and agency (Mulumba 2010), and even at times cope better in times of displacement compared to the males (Dolan 2009).

The stereotypical essentialization of women (adult and young) as "victims" and men as "perpetuators" of political violence and armed conflict assumes simplified definitions of such phenomena (Moser and Clark 2001). Treating both women and men as "objects" denies each their agency associated voice as actors in the process (Marchand and Parpart 1995). While young women experience sadness and pain, they at the same time reveal enormous courage during the conflict and remarkable resilience in its aftermath; they dispose high capacities of adaptability and resistance (Sommers 2006; Wessels 2006). It is therefore imperative to rhetorically listen to the voices of the young people, and understanding the meaning they derive from their lived experiences if peace and stability are to be attained. Taking young people's voices seriously means acknowledging their active participation in social life, their engagement within war and their suffering which continues during the post-conflict period (Olson in Boyden and Berry 2004). Alcoff (2006) notes that agency is a continuous process that should be assumed not only in the future but as an "ongoing feature of the past" (145). Women's Agency is complex since "women consent to, resist and reshape the social relations of power within a complex matrix of domination and subordination" (Fonow and Cook 2005: 2224), thus demanding interdisciplinary approaches.

I would like to note that my intention is not to totally reject Western theorization that points to youth in developing countries. I would, however, like to use such theories to deconstruct forms of Western domination of the third world, focusing on Africa. The youth bulge provides a case of a theory that is imperialistic, racist and strategically apportions blame to poor youth of color as responsible for global armed violence. Environmental, historical, political, and other situational circumstances that lead to anger of youth are thus downplayed which ends up underestimating the material effects these bring for the youth. I would also like to challenge the patriarchal oppression such theories (read youth bulge) and concepts (youth) cause for young women especially in situations of forced displacement. Western feminist theorizing especially from the women of color has been influential in understanding women's experiences in the third world through, for example, standpoint theory and Intersectionality. However, it is critical to emphasize indigenous theories and methodologies if specific experiences of women and girls encountering unique third world experiences that have not been considered in the Western world are to be recognized. I agree with Chilisa over the need to "rename the experiences of non-Western women from their standpoints" (2012: 270).

Youth participate both voluntarily and forcefully to sustain violent conflicts. It is imperative to appreciate that youth are social beings and they do not operate in a vacuum. The anger that young people manifest is a sign of underlying political and social tension usually grounded in class, race, ethnicity, poor economic situations, and political regimes in Africa (UNDP 2007). UNDP, further notes that societal crisis for instance facilitates easy access to small arms, cultural norms that support use of violence as an acceptable means of resolving conflict, and Africa's post-independence history of severe unrest and poverty. Critical too is the fact that while youth participate in violence, they are not the primary drivers (Hamilton 2007) but only tools used to attain the intended goals of the rebelling forces. While not downplaying Urdal's (2004) argument that youth bulges can increase the risk of armed conflict, I emphasize that male youth age and number cannot solely explain violence in developing countries. Youth are only caught up in societal crises due to poor governance, globalization, and other externally influenced causes including power struggles including economic factors, for instance, oil production. It is a combination of these that can be explosive. The UNDP (2007) report challenges stereotypical representations of African youth as violent emphasizing that it is the situation and environment created by colonialism, availability of small arms (all of which come from the developed world) and cultural break down that explain the region's unending conflicts. Blaming youth for the contemporary global violence is a way of avoiding to take responsibility for failed systems and structures as well as relegating the material effects created by historical events including slavery and colonialism and consequential effects like the creation of patriarchal societies (Smith 2005).

Class-based explanations of violence are in my perspective also strategically intended to maintain socioeconomic hierarchies that sustain white supremacy. Problematizing huge racialized populations creates the white race as being scarce. I believe it is relevant to explore and understand societal complexities that influence and inform individual behavior. Such complexities would include why communities continue to have growing populations despite population and fertility control measures globally promoted by the international community, why some youth choose to join rebel groups while others do not, why has unemployment persisted despite privatization and why African countries have kept in poverty despite the various IMF and World Bank policies implemented including the structural adjustment programs. Violence, therefore, in the feminist lens is a web of distinct yet connected structures, systems, processes, and practices that marginalize "othered" members (and elements) of community.

Conclusion

Understanding childhood and youthhood in Africa demands an examination of how young people are informing social transformation on the continent. Acknowledging their active participation only cannot fully explore the plight of young people and cannot explain the several failed frameworks for which no substantial results have been realized for the young people. Most importantly using adult experiences or children's experiences to inform youth and adolescent frameworks is the biggest challenge affecting the progress of youth in Africa. Youth intended programs should use the experiences of youth bearing in mind the different contexts and experiences they have encountered. Youth in post-conflict situations specifically have unique experiences and thus needs which deserve to be prioritized.

This chapter has critiqued the generalized understanding of numeric age as a line of difference between childhood and adulthood. I have argued that there is a middle ground comprising the characteristic features of both adulthood and childhood-youthhood. Disconnecting childhood from adulthood using age fails to acknowledge the processes of social change that happens in between, which is demonstrated in the youthhood stage. Age thus becomes a social shifter that is manipulated individually and collectively. Youth may view themselves as either children or adults depending on circumstances at play in a given space and time. They may at the same time consider themselves as both.

References

Alcoff, L. (2006). *Visible identities: Race, gender and self.* New York: Oxford University Press.

Boyden, J., & de Berry, J. (2004). *Children and youth on the front line: Ethnography, armed conflict and displacement.* New York: Berghahn Books.

Brainard, L., & Chollet, D. (Eds.). (2007). *Too poor for peace? Global poverty, conflict, and security in the 21st century.* Washington, DC: Brookings Institution.

Branch, A. (2007). Uganda's civil war and the politics of ICC intervention. *Ethics & International Affairs, 21*(2), 179–198.

Butler, J. (2010). *Frames of war: When is life grievable?* London and New York: Verso.

Chilisa, B. (2012). *Indigenous research methodologies.* Thousand Oaks: Sage.

Christiansen, C., Utas, M., & Vigh, H. E. (Eds.). (2006). *Navigating youth generating adulthood: Social becoming in an African context.* Uppsala: Nordiska Afrikainstitute.

Collins, H. P. (2000). *Black feminist thought: Knowledge, consciousness, and the politics of empowerment*. New York and London: Routledge.

Crenshaw, K. (1989). Demarginalizing the intersection of race and sex. *The University of Chicago Legal Forum, 140*, 139–167.

Crenshaw, K. W. (2012). From private violence to mass incarceration: Thinking intersectionally about women, race and social control. *UCLA Law Review, 59*, 1418–1472.

Dolan, C. (2009). *Social torture: The case of northern Uganda, 1986–2006*. New York and Oxford: Berghahn Books.

Fonow, M. M., & Cook, J. (2005). Feminist methodology: New Applications in the academy and public policy. *Signs, 30*(4), 2211–2236.

Hamilton, M. D. (2007). *The young and the restless: Examining incentives for youth participation in global conflict and development*. Paper presented at the annual meeting of the American Political Science Association, Chicago. http://citation.allacademic.com/meta/p210704_index.html.

Harding, S. (1993). Rethinking standpoint epistemology: What is strong objectivity. In L. Alcoff (Ed.), *Feminist epistemologies* (pp. 49–82). New York: Routledge.

Hendrixson, A. (2004). *The youth bulge: Defining the next generation young men as a threat to the future*. Population and development program, Hampshire College 19 (Winter, 2003).

Jaggar, A. M. (2008). *Just methods: An interdisciplinary feminist reader*. Boulder, CO: Paradigm Publishers.

Kabeer, N. (2008). *Paid work, women's empowerment and gender justice: Critical pathways of social change* (Pathways Working Paper 3). Retrieved June 3, 2016, from. http://www.lse.ac.uk/genderInstitute/about/resourcesNailaKabeer/kabeerPaidWorkWomensEmpowermentAndGenderJustice.pdf.

Kasozi, A. B. K. (2013). *The bitter bread of exile: The financial problems of sir Edward Mutesa 11 during his final exile, 1966–1969*. Kampala: Progressive Publishing House.

Marchand, M., & Parpart, J. (1995). *Feminism, post modernism, development*. New York: Routledge.

Mesquida, C., & Wiener, N. (1999). Male age composition and conflict severity. *Political and Life Science, 18*(2), 181–189. Beech Tree Publishing.

Million, D. (2009). Felt theory: An indigenous feminist approach to affect and history. *Wicazo Review, 24*(2), 53–76. Project Muse.

Morrow, V. (2013). What's in a number? Unsettling the boundaries of age. *Childhood, 20*, 151–155. https://doi.org/10.1177/0907568213484199.

Moser, C., & Clark, F. (2001). *Victims, perpetuators or actors? Gender, armed conflict and political violence*. New York: Zed books.

Mulumba, D. (2010). *Changing fortunes: Women's economic opportunities in post war northern Uganda*. Investing in peace, 3(September). International Alert.

Namuggala V. F. (2017). *Gambling, dancing, sex work: Notions of youth employment in Uganda*. Brighton: Institute of Development Studies Press, University of Sussex.

National Youth Policy. (2001). The national youth policy: A vision for youth in the 21st century. *Ministry of Gender, Labour and Social Development.* Kampala, The Republic of Uganda. http://www.youthpolicy.org/national/Uganda_2001_National_Youth_Policy.pdf.

Oyewumi, O. (1997). *The invention of women: Making an African sense of western gender discourses.* Minneapolis: University of Minnesota Press.

Rogers, M. et al. (2007). The role of religious fundamentalism in terrorist violence: A social psychological analysis. *The International Review of Psychiatry Special Issue on Mass Violence and Mental Health, 19*(3), 253–262.

Shepherd, L. (2008). *Gender, violence and security: Discourse as practice.* London: Zed Books.

Sjoberg, L. (2013). *Gendering global conflict: Toward a feminist theory of war.* New York: Columbia University Press.

Sjoberg, L. (2014). *Gender, war and conflict.* Cambridge: Polity Press.

Smith, A. (2005). *Conquest: Sexual violence and American Indian genocide.* Cambridge: South End Press.

Smith, A. (2006). Heteropatriarchy and the three pillars of settler colonialism. In A. Smith, B. Richie, J. Sudbury, & J. White (Eds.), *The color of violence: The INCITE* (pp. 68–73). Cambridge: South End Press.

Sommers, M. (2006). *Fearing Africa's young men—The case of Rwanda* (Social Development Papers: Conflict Prevention and Reconstruction. No. 32).

Sommers, M. (2007). Embracing the margins: Working with youth amid war & insecurity. In L. Brainard & D. Chollet (Eds.), *Too poor for peace? Global poverty, conflict, and security in the 21st Century.* Washington, DC: Brookings Institution.

Sommers, M. (2011). Governance, security and culture: Assessing Africa's youth bulge. *International Journal of Conflict and Violence, 5*(2), 292–303.

UNDP. (2007). *The youth of Africa: A threat to security or a force for peace?* Conference Background Paper. http://www.genevadeclaration.org.

Urdal, H. (2004). The devil in the demographics: The effect of youth bulges on domestic armed conflict, (1950–2000). *Social Development Papers, Conflict Prevention and Reconstruction, 14.*

Urdal, H. (2006). A clash of generations? Youth bulges and political violence. *International Studies Quarterly, 50,* 607–630.

Urdal, H., Tadjoeddin, M. Z., Murshed, S. M., & Strand, H. (2011). Population pressure, horizontal inequality and political violence: A disaggregated study of Indonesian provinces, 1990–2003. *The Journal of Development Studies, 47*(3), 377–398.

Wessels, M. (2006). *Child soldiers: From violence to protection.* Cambridge and London: Harvard University Press.

Wibben, A. (2011). *Feminist security studies: A narrative approach.* London and New York: Routledge.

CHAPTER 6

Girlhood, Violence, and Humanitarian Assistance

Introduction

This chapter focuses on the humanitarian assistance as a major component of survival during situations of distress and displacement. Despite its contribution in saving lives, humanitarian assistance has its own controversies especially from the perspective of the beneficiaries. This chapter centers on such complexities focusing on the experiences of young women in northern Uganda. This chapter examines the nature of aid provided and how recipients conceptualize it, the gendered experiences involved and the sociocultural dynamics that inform the implementation of humanitarian assistance. Using the case of northern Uganda, the chapter concludes that humanitarian assistance at times facilitates violenceViolence, particularly against young women. This is due to humanitarian operation through cultural patriarchal dominant structures that sustain power hierarchies in favor of men.

In situations of armed conflict and displacement, livelihoods are destroyed which makes humanitarian assistance essential for survival (Kalin et al. 2010). Northern Uganda experienced armed violence for over two decades, which made humanitarian aid essential for human survival. Conflict scholars have, however, described the Northern Uganda situation as the "world's worst humanitarian crises" (Dolan and Hovil 2006: 1). This crisis was characterized by starvation, sexual violence, survival sex, beatings, detention, arrest, and torture of civilians

(Dolan 2009). Humanitarian assistance, therefore, contributed (and continues to contribute) to saving lives by providing the basic human survival needs including food, shelter, and medication and other social services including education (Gelsdorf et al. 2002).

Humanitarian assistance was provided both during the conflict and in post-conflict settings with the overarching aim of ending human suffering and saving lives. This chapter, therefore, acknowledges the contribution such aid makes. At the same time, the chapter also observes the negative aspects attributed to humanitarian assistance. Humanitarian assistance, for instance, at times initiates and/or sustains violence within and among the population it targets. In northern Uganda, a large portion of the violence landed on marginalized groups especially women and girl children. Harrell-Bond (1986), explains that the perspective of the beneficiaries is very crucial in understanding humanitarian assistance's limitations. This chapter therefore uses this approach to examine humanitarian assistance in northern Uganda largely drawing on the perspective of formerly displaced returned young people.

Scholars, activists, and practitioners acknowledge the inevitable demand for humanitarian assistance as a consequence of armed violence (Dolan 2009). In the case of northern Uganda, the region escalated into a severe humanitarian crisis due to a simultaneous occurrence of a number of factors. First, the war led to thousands of people being killed, others injured, and millions displaced (Soto 2009). Besides the civil war, natural disasters particularly drought and floods also hit northern Uganda exacerbating livelihoods and creating an increased burden toward population vulnerability (Smith 2012). Additionally, famine and diseases equally troubled the region during the decades of the armed violence. A combination of the above resulted in local, regional, and global disturbances in the form of internally displaced persons (IDPs), refugees, and violations of basic human rights (Branch 2007; Dolan 2009; Tim and Vlassenroot 2010). This explains the acute humanitarian conditions in northern Uganda, described to be the most persistent and deadliest Complex Humanitarian Emergencies (CHEs) in the world (Spitzer and Twikirize 2013). The desire to end such human suffering and improve survival informs the principles of humanitarian aid and assistance.

The already daring situation in the northern part of Uganda has been recently worsened by the inflow of refugees from neighboring countries. Majority of these refugees are children. World Vision (2017) notes that of the two thousand (2000) refugees estimated to arrive each day, nearly

60% are children hence describing the situation as "children's crisis". Such children are unaccompanied, tired, malnourished, and in most cases sick. It is common for children in situations of violence to lose contact with their caretakers and hence rely heavily on humanitarian agencies for survival. Children are the most vulnerable and thus in dire need of assistance. While intended to end and/or alleviate human suffering, humanitarian assistance in northern Uganda has resulted in and/or perpetuated violence within the return communities. Individual community members were affected differently based on their gender and age, marital, and motherhood statuses among other factors. In this chapter, I center the discussion on the experiences of young women in "post-conflict" northern Uganda. I explore how violence against young women occurs along a continuum of cultural, political, and humanitarian processes that are implemented in the region. Female children marginalized by the aforementioned patriarchal structures thus experience the worst forms of violence in both the private and public spheres.

In order to understand the impact humanitarian assistance has on the experiences of young women, we must understand what constitutes assistance. I briefly explain the principles underlying this approach to human experiences of distress and how these globally held principles affect local experiences. I then contextualize what humanitarian assistance means in relation to this specific study. To do this I discuss the nature of the assistance provided and how respondents conceptualize it, the gendered experiences involved, as well as the sociocultural dynamics that inform the implementation of humanitarian assistance. I, then, examine how assistance initiates and sustains violence especially against young women. I later acknowledge and discuss the challenges that providers encounter. I specifically focus on the humanitarian programs run by the nongovernmental agencies since these dominate the implementation of humanitarian services in northern Uganda.

Overview and Understanding of Humanitarian Assistance

Humanitarian assistance is a survival mechanism for both civilians and armed forces. It is, therefore, necessary to familiarize oneself with the central principles informing assistance, how it is defined and how it is practically implemented at the grassroots, drawing on the northern Uganda experience. Humanitarian assistance refers to activities aimed at addressing the needs of people affected by emergencies. Such activities involve actions designed to save lives, end human suffering, maintain and protect human dignity during and in the aftermath of disasters, and prevent disaster re-occurrences (Global Humanitarian Assistance Report 2016). Fundamentally, humanitarian assistance has four major principles: humanity, impartiality, neutrality, and independence (OCHA 2011). The overarching mandate is to end human suffering irrespective of political, religious, cultural, and other varying ideologies particular individuals might hold. While researchers and implementers generally understand and accept aid as such, at the same time humanitarian assistance is dynamic and varies from situation-to-situation. It is thus context specific especially in implementation strategies to address the specific concerns intended recipients might have. Assistance is ideally context specific, need-based, and locally grounded.

Despite situational variances, recovery assistance's goal is to support affected communities toward management of own recovery. To do this, humanitarian agencies supplement personal, family, and community structures that are disrupted during insurgencies. While community management of its own recovery is central for reconstruction, scholars have noted that in northern Uganda, returning populations have been treated as "passive victims" (Dolan 2009: 25) and thus mere recipients of aid provided. Consequently, humanitarian processes and programs have overlooked concerns that are considered critical from a local perspective.

In its glossary of humanitarian terms, Relief Web describes assistance as aid provided to address "the physical, material, and legal needs of persons of concern. This may include food items, medical supplies, clothing, shelter, seeds and tools, as well as the provision of infrastructure, such as schools and roads" (Relief Web 2008: 12). Conceptualizing human suffering solely in the form of physical and material effects, however, misrepresents the critical elements of humanity that inform what happens physically—the emotions (Sjoberg 2013). I thus argue that the nonmaterial needs and effects are just as valid as material ones, and thus both deserve equal consideration during reconstruction for sustainable peace. It is thus crucial to adopt a holistic understanding of humanitarian assistance to include the emotional, spiritual, psychological, and environmental concerns of the communities engulfed in such situations. Such an approach would limit violence resulting from and perpetuated by aid especially in the post-conflict phase.

Humanitarian assistance in Uganda has been externally informed, funded, and implemented, relying on dominant Western concepts and theories to explain the situation, and impose meaning on communities in northern Uganda. Concepts like youth, child mothers, child soldiers, and child-headed households are all external constructions used in northern Uganda. Even the understanding of other critical concepts like children, adults, family, and vulnerability are largely grounded in the dominant Western view. This has led to different understandings on the part of the humanitarian programs and the local population. Putting the above definitional limitations into consideration, I rely on a broader definition of humanitarian recovery assistance, which stretches beyond the traditional understanding described earlier. I include critical psychological, economic and social support aspects of both in the short, medium, and long term. According to this definition, humanitarian recovery assistance prioritizes assistance aimed at immediate/short-term needs (i.e. during the displacement) and the strategic/long-term needs (conceptualized as recovery assistance in the post-conflict stage).

Recovery on the other hand in this study constitutes the "process of rebuilding, restoring and rehabilitating the community following an emergency or disaster, continuing until the disruption has been rectified, demands on services have been returned to normal levels, and the needs of those affected have been met" (Emergency, Response and Recovery 2010: 101). In the case of northern Uganda, however, the historical processes that amounted to unbalanced regional development and political domination by the southern region had already disrupted the region. This dual disruption—before and after the conflict, necessitated development-oriented programs for both the formerly displaced as well as the entire populace.

UGANDA AND HUMANITARIAN ASSISTANCE

Uganda has had a violent history especially in the post-independence stage and has for long been a recipient of humanitarian assistance. More recently, between 2001 and 2010, Uganda received USD1.17 billion in humanitarian assistance (Smith 2012). Since 2006, the United States has been the largest humanitarian aid donor to Uganda, and European Union institutions have collectively been the second largest, giving a total of US$231.5 million and US$178.2 million, respectively (ibid.).

While this assistance is instrumental, as explained by the humanitarian principle to end human suffering, it has been misallocated and in some instances misappropriated by the government of Uganda. The major central government reaction to the over two-decade civil war has been to augment the military budget. This increased military spending, however, has not resulted in positive trends towards peace (Dolan 2009) but rather led to more displacement and encampment. Assistance is thus crucial for formerly displaced persons in northern Uganda as a way of facilitating self-sustenance. In this section, I discuss how assistance programs in northern Uganda emerged from universal humanitarian assistance frameworks. Understanding this connection helps to explain the decisions made relating to assistance, as well as how these decisions have affected local contexts and perspectives in northern Uganda.

The post-conflict phase in northern Uganda started in October 2008 when the President of Uganda, Yoweri Museveni, ordered the closure of IDPs camps (IDMC 2008). This closure was supported by the local community officials who took on initiatives targeting the IDPs "pushing for returns to be speeded up, including by threatening imminent demolition of huts or leveling of the camp" (155) in case the population did not vacate. Such local support was rooted in selfish needs of the leaders who wanted to use the land on which camps had been established due to land scarcity in the region (Kindi 2010). O'Callaghan and Gilbride (2008) explain that local leaders used humanitarian assistance as a tool to mobilize IDPs to leave the camps, despite returnees' anxiety about insecurity, social services, and uncertainty of livelihood in the return areas. One of the key elements of conflict resolution and reintegration is voluntary return/assisted voluntary return. Under this policy, returnees must be sure that the concerns that caused their displacement have been resolved and the areas of return no longer pose a threat or any sense of fear (International Organization for Migration 2012). In northern Uganda, however, the policy of voluntary return[1] was not followed since local leadership pressurized and persuaded IDPs to return to their villages using humanitarian assistance as bait. Important to note also is that

---

[1] Voluntary Return and Reintegration is an indispensable part of a comprehensive approach to migration management aiming at orderly and humane return and reintegration of migrants who are unable or unwilling to remain in the host countries and thus wish to voluntarily return to their countries of origin (International Organization for Migration), http://iom.by/en/activities/assisted-voluntary-return-and-reintegration. While this is focused on refugees, this policy also applies to IDPs who move within national borders.

besides their selfish interests, leaders were also pressured by the central government to enforce return of the communities (Dolan 2009).

Due to the sudden closure of camps, return areas were not adequately prepared to receive the formerly displaced people. The areas were inhabitable and insecure for instance due to bombs that remained planted in the bushes, domestic violence, and rape. The sudden return also worsened the already vulnerable health conditions leading to disease outbreaks like malaria, diarrhea, and cholera (Annan et al. 2011). This situation continues and does not show signs of ending any time soon, given the enormous destruction rendered during the conflict. As a result, these returned communities live in absolute poverty; institutional operations and services are hampered by poor infrastructure, lack qualified personnel, and have limited self-sustenance within the communities.

All recovery programs implemented in northern Uganda were under the Peace, Recovery Development Plan (PRDP) that sought to streamline the rebuilding of the war-affected part of the northern region and consolidate peace and development (OPM 2007). Implementation of PRDP was effected in 2009, with a budget of US$600 million for Northern Uganda. The plan had four strategic objectives: "consolidation of state authority; rebuilding and empowering communities; revitalizing the economy and peace-building and reconciliation" (Smith 2012: 14). PRDP also included programs specific to regions affected by the conflict: Agricultural Livelihood Recovery Project for Northern Uganda (ALREP), Northern Uganda Social Action Fund (NUSAF), Northern Uganda Rehabilitation Program (NUREP), Karamoja Livelihoods Program (KALIP), and Northern Uganda Transition Initiative (NUTI). While these are good programs, operating in isolation from the local initiatives has limited their effectiveness (Ochen et al. 2012).

THE NATURE OF ASSISTANCE PROVIDED TO RETURNING POPULATIONS

To get a clear perspective of humanitarian assistance and the impact it has on the formerly displaced communities, it is imperative to scrutinize the characteristics of assistance provided. Such analysis is critical to understanding the gendered roles, responsibilities, expectation, and entitlements of individuals within communities. It also helps to appreciate how assistance can differ in form, time, and space. The discussion also includes aspects to do with quantity, quality, and sustainability. This facilitates the acknowledgement of community agency and resilience by analyzing their survival amidst shortage and lack of basic needs among other constraints.

In northern Uganda, humanitarian programs distributed assistance to formerly displaced communities in the form of immediate needs like food items including maize flour, millet flour, and beans. Other immediate needs included household items like blankets, water cans, and mosquito nets. Immediate needs were provided with the intention of solving the daily survival needs of the communities, for instance, those that prevent starvation, malnutrition, and in extreme cases, death. Three-month startup food packages were given to returning families to enable them resettle. The packages were being provided on the assumption that the short-term maturing crops planted would be ready to continue providing families with food and avoid starvation after the startup food packages were exhausted. This assumption, however, did not come to pass. Floods badly hit farms, severely eroding people's young gardens, which created further vulnerabilities to the returned populations.

Besides the direct food package, humanitarian food assistance was also pegged to individuals who first accessed services, such as education, health, and reproductive health. This was intended to encourage use of such services. The conflict in northern Uganda coupled with the prolonged stay in the IDP camps had severely crippled the systems for access to services, such as education, health, and reproductive health that preexisted. Because of changed attitudes and increased levels of hopelessness that displaced persons had developed as a result of the conflict, individuals were unwilling to access services even when and where they did exist. Food, however, required for survival, the settling IDPs would go where it was provided. As such food assistance was distributed in several forms namely; Food for Education (FFE), and Food for Health (FFH). FFE was distributed in form of food for school-going children with the aim of reducing malnutrition and also as a onetime package at the end of the term (three months of school) depending on attendance. This was intended to encourage regular attendance and thus children's retention in school. FFH was distributed to pregnant and lactating mothers who attended antenatal and postnatal care, respectively. The major aim was to encourage women to seek medical services as a way of reducing maternal and infant mortality rates. All these were good programs but ended up having gendered and age-specific limitations, as this chapter will demonstrate.

In addition to food aid and other day-to-day needs, assistance also included supplies intended for agricultural sustenance. These were in the form of improved variety seeds including maize, beans, groundnuts, and pineapples among others. The seeds and plants were to be planted in order to improve food security, through increased food production initially for household consumption but also for sale in case of surplus production. Humanitarian agencies also distributed animals especially goats and cattle. The animals were to improve nutrition through the provision of milk and meat as well as sale of products for cash to cater for other basic needs. Oxen and ox ploughs were also provided for plowing the land. While this was a good step to community self sustainability, the recipients noted some limitations. For instance, communities culturally do not consume goat milk, which decreased the nutrition value anticipated by the humanitarian providers. Unlike the local breeds, crossbreed goats also were difficult and expensive to maintain given the harsh conditions and bad weather. Goats in addition are not valued as part of bride price, an issue some returnees struggled with. Bride price in northern Uganda largely means cattle and while other animals like goats can be taken for cultural weddings, they are just additional items. The provision of goats by humanitarian agencies disregarded the cultural inclinations of the local population, which in turn limited the anticipated impact of assistance.

In northern Uganda, cattle being the backbone of their culture in terms of wealth, marriage, farm production through animal plowing, and nutrition through consumption of cow milk, the locals perceived assistance in the form of improved milk from goats as a deliberate effort aimed at destroying the local culture. The intended beneficiaries thus put up much resistance to this form of assistance by for instance discouraging one another from receiving such aid or selling it off immediately it was received. One participant explained that:

> The goats are improved breeds. They are so delicate, require a lot of attention and cannot withstand the drought seasons. Also here we rear goats for meat and not milk. Some people sell them but still the resale value is low.

The use of oxen for plowing was on the other hand a masculine role, which women were not expected to perform in addition to lack of skills. Women who received oxen, therefore, had to hire men to plough their gardens, which made production more expensive for the female farmers.

Many men, on the other hand, could not imagine or even tolerate being employed by a woman.

Humanitarian assistance likewise focused on skills training for returning IDPs. Agencies distributed assistance in the form of scholastic materials, and vocational training for school-going children and youth. While the previous two categories (food and agricultural inputs) target families, scholastic materials were more individualized to the most marginalized children. The government of Uganda provides free access to primary and secondary education in government-sponsored schools through Universal Primary Education (UPE) and Universal Secondary Education (USE), respectively. However, though the service is free, the government does not cater for personal needs and meals at school. Humanitarian assistance, therefore, greatly facilitated the enrollment, retention, and performance of children in schools by providing scholastic materials like books, pens, pencils, uniforms, and lunch for the students considered to be most vulnerable.

Essential to note is that the interpretation of marginalization was different for both humanitarian programs and the local community. Programs, for instance, classified former child soldiers and children from female-headed households generally as the most marginalized. While these are highly vulnerable, communities alternately identified the most marginalized as those members with limited community networks, for instance, those considered to be haunted by the spirits (psychologically tortured), children who had no access to land and abandoned or unaccompanied minors. While the majority of the haunted (traumatized) are child soldiers, the communities do not perceive all child soldiers as haunted and thus should not be prioritized for special attention. The communities identified the haunted as those children whose hands were stained with human blood and were not in good terms with the spirits and the departed. Given their state of mind, such children were isolated and outcast by the community, hence necessitating prioritized support. Yet, the program implementers did not take community evaluations into account and thus the communities did not believe the programs facilitated the recovery of the most affected children.

Some agencies, however, implemented programs in partnership with communities. This ensured sustainability and a sense of ownership from the local community. Humanitarian agencies, for instance, provided communal services through the construction and rehabilitation of schools, roads, and health centers, boreholes, and water tanks. While earlier scholars noted limited community involvement in programs (Ochen et al. 2012), this study realized some improvement; community members partnered with reconstruction programs in various forms including offering time and labor during construction of such infrastructure. Others provided building materials in form of bricks, timber, and grass. Others on the other hand provided land on which such infrastructure was established.

Community involvement and participation, however, had gendered and age implications. For instance, women highlighted that providing labor at construction sites increased their workload and thus hours spent working. To encounter this challenge, young women had to take on more roles in the domestic space to relieve the elders. This was because men did not get involved in domestic chores. It thus meant women had to wake up earlier than usual to finish up the domestic chores before joining the communal commitments. From the local perspective, one is expected to participate in community roles to be considered a good resident. So, women had no choice but to work triple roles. In their guide to gender-analysis framework, March et al. (1999) classified the roles into three major categories—reproductive, productive, and communal roles. Culturally, construction of houses is a feminine role that involves identifying, cutting, carrying and laying of grass, and other building materials. However, the role of building in the public space (e.g. of schools and hospitals) is not culturally explained. And since it involved rewards in the form of assistance items including food, men were more willing to participate. This is because as Dolan (2009) explains, men had a lot of free time compared to women. In addition, the men control women's bodies, freedom of movement, as well as their time and how they allocate it. On the other hand, such humanitarian initiatives did not include children at all. Child-headed households thus missed out despite encountering the same challenges as adult households.

The overview above provides a perspective for analyzing the violence instigated and perpetuated by assistance. The violence ranges from individual to group, private to public, as well as structural and institutional level forms of violence. While different, all these forms of violence are interconnected in form and draw from each other.

Girlhood and Violence

Academics, activists and policymakers acknowledge the global challenge presented by violence against women and girls (WHO 2013). While violence transcends geographical, economic, racial, religious, and age boundaries, it is more profound in the developing world and exacerbated during situations of humanitarian emergencies such as armed conflict (McKay 2004; McKay and Mazurana 2004; Moortz et al. 2017). Even when such crises end, complex brutal cultures of violence persist especially in relation to gender-based violence (Jones-Casey et al. 2014).

Conflict scholars have noted that violence inevitably initiates, perpetuates or results from war (Christie et al. 2001). It takes various levels including the individual, family and structural violence. This chapter prioritizes structural violence since it encompasses all the other forms. Paying specific attention to humanitarian aid, I take on Galtung's (1969) description of structural violence as a type of violence which corresponds with the systemic ways in which a given social structure or social institution prevents individuals or groups from meeting basic needs. Specifically, I use the concept "structural violence" to refer to how systems, structures, institutions, and processes operate to marginalize young women as a specific group with unique needs and concerns. By failing to acknowledge their unique position, humanitarian frameworks affect young women's access to and use of resources and services including education and health, and deny them control over their bodies and sexual rights. I discuss local and international organizations, religious, and cultural humanitarian frameworks as initiating and perpetuating violence against young people centering on experiences of young women.

In addition, systemic frameworks, institutions, and structures through which humanitarian agencies operated also inform the regularity and severity of violence individuals in northern Uganda face. Such institutions include the police, schools, and health centers. A direct link therefore exists between institutionalized and structural violence, and violence against women and girls, especially those in situations of armed violence like northern Uganda. Giving special attention to northern Uganda, Chris Dolan for instance notes that "there is a crucial connection to be made between state-level dynamics and micro-level behavior, and the ideas which make up masculinity are a key connector between the two" (2002: 60). While violence has persisted, government has not been entirely passive. Some critical steps have been taken to combat violence against women and girls all over Uganda but also in the northern part of the country. Uganda therefore has strong policy frameworks supporting gender equality.

GOVERNMENT EFFORTS TO COMBAT VIOLENCE AGAINST WOMEN AND GIRLS

The government of Uganda has taken important steps to improve the position of women and girls through policies geared toward gender equality. Uganda is signatory to numerous international human rights treaties explicitly prohibiting gender based violence including UN International Convention on Civil and Political Rights (ICCPR), the UN Convention Against Torture and other cruel, inhuman and degrading treatment or punishment (CAT), and the African Charter on Human and People's Rights (ACHPR). A lot however, still needs to be done in the domestication and implementation of such treaties. In her statement, Rukia Isanga Nakadama[2] noted that the Government of Uganda "declared zero tolerance to violence against women" and has taken on various strategies to commit to its declaration. Among the various strategies are legal measures like the domestic violence act (2010), the prohibition of female genital mutilation (2010), prevention of the trafficking in persons act (2009), and a child and family protection unit at police stations. In specific relation to armed conflict, Uganda is signatory to UNSCR 1325 and 1820 that call for ending violence against women and increasing their participation in peace-building initiatives.

While the policies and legal frameworks are in place, implementation, and localization (cultural appropriateness) of such frameworks is limited (CEDOVIP 2016; Cheney 2007). Through this study, I too found this conclusion valid in post-conflict northern Uganda. Women and girls face several forms of gendered violence intersecting in various ways and at different levels including individual and societal. These maintain power hierarchies and perpetrate violence against culturally and socially marginalized groups especially young women and children (Chai et al. 2016; Kerker et al. 2015).

---

[2] She was the Minister of State for Gender, labor and social development. She made the remark during the 57th session of the United Nations Commission on the status of women on March 5, 2013 in New York. http://www.un.org/womenwatch/daw/csw/csw57/generaldiscussion/memberstates/uganda.pdf.

The policies and treaties signed by the central government do not seem to address the specific needs of northern Uganda. Neither are these government frameworks included in the post-conflict reconstruction guidelines, which government calls on all humanitarian implementers to adapt. Where gender is mentioned, it is treated as a binary between men and women, disregarding critical aspects gender relates with including age, as well as intra-group power dynamics particular categories experience. The bottom line to all this is continued violence especially against young women who are intersectionally disadvantaged by their gender, age, class, marital status, and reproductive capabilities among other things especially in the post-conflict setting.

Post-conflict Conditions Contributing to Violence Against Young Women

In northern Uganda, there is a general lack of resources. This gives an upper hand to area operating NGOs, religious (Christian) and state programs to intervene on their own terms in the lives of the returned communities because the resources they provide are on high demand. Limited resources, in turn, affect allocations geared toward protection of women and girls. This was especially the case for sexual violence in the return areas where various sectors involved in maintaining justice largely disadvantage women and girls. Participants reported that in some few cases where legal procedures were taken and the culprits convicted, the result was imprisonment. However, for the culprit to remain in custody before judgment was passed, the complainant was required to cater for the perpetrator's stay by way of providing food. Otherwise, the suspects would be released due to lack of basic supplies at the police stations. Given the food insecurity in the region, victims often gave up on reporting rape cases even when the rapist was known, because they lacked the means to support the perpetrators while in police custody. After experiencing terrible frustration related to this, Atim lamented:

> They (police) asked me for food for the prisoner. But we barely had enough for the family. They let him (rapist) go since I could not feed him and the police could not feed him either. I understand they cannot starve someone in custody. But why would I feed that man (rapist)? I think he gave them something.

Food is a basic need that should ideally be readily available but in situations of distress it becomes a significant issue upon which serious decisions are based. Several studies have focused on the limited reporting of sexual harassment cases (Human Rights Watch 2005; Refugee Documentation Center 2010) but this is not the case here. Atim reported with evidence and available witnesses that she had been raped. The police took up the case but later contacted her to feed the inmate if he was to be held till trial. Although a trial ideally would occur within 48 hours according to the 1995 constitution of the Republic of Uganda, this is rarely the case given the backlog of cases. As Atim explains in the quote above, they "barely had enough for the family" and could not afford to feed another person for an unstipulated period of time, moreover a rapist. This is a major structural challenge to which the state contributes. Even though the state is signatory to various intervention frameworks to prevent violence against women, their commitment to implement actual intervention is still lacking. Recovery assistance thus needs to strategically address sexual-and gender-based violence by for instance improving services in such institutional frameworks.

Besides the national structural challenges, the specific state institutions too have particular limitations. Atim in the quote above notes, "I think he gave them something". This, in the local context reflects a bribe, indicating a common assumption that the police officers prioritize personal selfish ends over social justice. This is not surprising for many Ugandans given the consistent annual rankings of the Uganda police as the most corrupt government institution with a bribery rate of 48% by 2012 (Namulondo 2012). Having recovery assistance directed toward providing services that promote social justice would therefore improve the status of young women in northern Uganda.

The lack of specific programs targeting female youth intersectional nature increases their vulnerability and dependency on especially men but also older women. Men exploit such vulnerability and employ intimidation as a way of controlling and dominating women further. Some responses revealed that men, for instance, threaten to marry another wife if the wives cannot offer sex or do not bear as many babies as men want. While adultery and polygamy is common and not a valid reason for divorce according to the Teso cultural socialization, women admit it is hurting and threatening knowing that you are responsible for your husband's extramarital relations. Men, therefore, blame women for their sexual (mis)conduct as a way of justifying it to women, their families and the community. Husbands in such cases are operating in cultural traditions that disregard women's consent to sexual intercourse and general reproductive justice. Attaching aid to headship of households, therefore, facilitates men's control over women. Women as a result live in fear, suspicion, and jealousy of each other, which affects their ability to collectively work together to challenge the obstacles they encounter. Intimidation also involves the use of abusive and insulting language against women. This lowers their self-esteem and creates more dependency on men. One respondent, Acio—a 26-year-old mother of five lived in the camp for nine years and lost both her parents during the war. She had this to say while referring to her husband:

> It is like he made a song out of it. He always tells me I am useless, I have no family and the day he will chase me out of his house, I will live on the street. He reminds me of how he helped me when I had nothing and gave me where to stay… this marriage is good for nothing; he says he was just helping me.

Such comments result in young women internalizing marginalization and violence and accepting it as normal and expectable. Culturally, it is very important that a person identifies with a particular family and community as social security. In the case of Acio, she is constantly reminded of how she has nowhere to turn to. Not having a family, therefore, compels Acio and her children to stay with her abusive husband because it gives them a sense of belonging. As such she is compelled to work towards the approval of the husband and not her own self. She provides another example of how women give up themselves for the sake of the family and children.

Humanitarian agencies, in addition, apply a language that does not reflect the lived realities of local communities returning from displacement. As a way of categorizing the population, humanitarian agencies have unconsciously labeled and "othered" some sections of the population. Agencies refer for instance to under-age combatants as "child-soldiers" and under-age mothers as "child mothers". In the local context, such terminologies have lasting impacts on labeled individual's entitlement and worthiness. Communities perceive such individuals as unworthy and undeserving of protection, love, and other services as compared to other "normal" community members. One respondent expressed dissatisfaction with humanitarian assistance concentration on what agencies termed the most vulnerable—child soldiers. She said,

> Why are they receiving all the care? It is them that have caused harm to us yet they are being favored by the help programs [as she termed them]. We suffered in the camp and now in the return areas. I just don't think the programs know what those people did.

It is telling that this participant refers to them as people and not child soldiers. This culturally would mean these individuals can be held accountable for their actions. According to this respondent, these people lost their naivety and they are not children to be protected and provided for like the humanitarian agencies are doing. Irrespective of the conditions under which individuals get involved in these socially stigmatized practices, for instance through abductions into armed forces and forced prostitution, society judges them. One female youth aged between 23 and 25 explained the dilemma she encountered upon return to her village.

> Yes I was abducted but I was confined and I did not kill anyone. I did not even hold a gun. I was married off and used to cook for others during the abduction... when we came back, people think we are all murderers and heartless. Neighbors mistreated me and no one wanted to talk to me. That's how I joined some other friends and we went to the center (town center), and later started prostitution for food, money and other needs.

The community labeling this girl as a murderer resulted in her failure to reintegrate and cope due to stigmatization, discrimination, and eventual isolation. The search for belonging in post-conflict settings, however, comes amidst limited alternative choices. Prostitution is not a good alternative because it also is undervalued and judged by the community but at least she has friends to support her and can also earn basic needs. This case demonstrates how public communal biases result in individualized violence by limiting access to humanitarian access.

Humanitarian agencies need to work with marginalized individuals as relational beings. I wish to note that survival in this particular area (just like many other African settings) depends on communal relations. As such, failing to be recognized as an accepted community member highly affects those individuals who are negatively labeled. Consequently, they search for new communities that will accommodate them. Girls therefore end up taking on risky and at times life-threatening ventures that marginalize them even more. Like the quote above demonstrates, for such young women, prostitution is the only available choice for their survival. But while immediate and daily needs are met, survival sex consequently results in long-term consequences including unwanted pregnancies, and sexually transmitted infections including HIV. While prostitution enables survival, such sex, in the long run, decreases one's chances of survival, especially when coupled with poor health service provision in (northern) Uganda. One respondent—a young woman and mother of four noted:

> People think because we get money from sex, we are not good people. But we use that very money to provide for our families, our children. If I cannot acquire basic needs like food for my children, what do you expect me to do? This is the only alternative…Prostitution booms at the end of the month when government employees (soldiers) receive salary… we are criticized for being loose but no one criticizes us for putting food on the table.

These young women sell sexual services not for selfish interests (personal pleasure) as the general community puts it, but rather, as a sacrifice they make for their own survival and that of their dependents. Foregoing prostitution would mean starvation and probably death for not only these women, but also those under their care including children, elderly, the differently abled, and other members of the family. I, therefore, find it critical to emphasize the selflessness these young women portray. They prioritize their families and especially children and not themselves, to the extent that they involve themselves in economic activities that are harmful to them for the sake of providing for their families. Humanitarian agencies need to front the contribution such individuals make and use it as a basis for their support rather than capitalizing on the negatively perceived communal aspects.

In African feminist epistemologies (Chilisa 2012), motherhood is a key aspect that comes along with status, as well as roles, responsibilities, obligations, and sacrifice. This reflects what African feminist Njoki Wane observed in her study among Mbu women in Kenya that "African women act: they don't sit and watch their children starve" (2003: 17). Women's "acting" in northern Uganda has been hindered by lack of viable alternatives hence offering sex in return for food and money despite communal disapproval.

Analyzed from a gendered perspective, all blame is put on the female youth and not the government soldiers, businessmen, and other males in the community who pay for the sexual services these young women offer. This gendered blaming pathologizes young women as moral transgressors. Communities believe that such humanitarian services should be benefiting only "acceptable" or "descent" members of their community. Such perception is extended and applied by the community and their leaders in identifying who merits benefits from humanitarian programs. As such, the needs, concerns, and views of the socially "othered" are downplayed since these (mostly young) women are believed to have made the choice to live such immoral lives. The categorizations largely informed by humanitarian programming therefore entrenches the marginalization young women face by creating a cultural conflict with the humanitarian assistance operations.

Besides labeling, humanitarian assistance also perpetuates violence through exclusion and/or omission. In northern Uganda, there is no specific term to refer to young women/female youth. As a result, implementation of humanitarian assistance programs is faced with the challenge of reaching out to and categorization of female youth/young women. Humanitarian assistance programs use the term youth to refer to both male and female. For communities, this term really denotes young men; hence males dominate youth aid groups both as members and leaders. Divergences of understanding who constitutes a youth, hinders young women from accessing assistance leading to sexual exploitation by group leaders and humanitarian implementers in return for inclusion into the humanitarian assistance programs. One girl said,

> Leaders favor their girlfriends. They benefit from every project that comes. They are registered first. When you do not offer them what they want [sex], then your benefit is limited". Another elaborated how "girls fight over those men with connections to aid. Especially if it is the leaders who register us on behalf of the organizations, and the implementers from organizations who work as field coordinators.

Culturally among the Ateso (the largest tribal community group in the study area besides the Kumam) one is either a child or an adult. Although the concept youth has been adopted it has been locally perceived to refer to young men only, thus leaving out females. As such, even when programs include female youth, the females tend to disassociate themselves with the categorization of youth given the negative attributes attached to it including promiscuity, rebelliousness and violence.

The violence young women experience can be understood and also explained in both feminist and indigenous perspectives. "Early adulthood" for instance is now culturally perceived as a survival strategy for females in the post-conflict areas. Given the food shortages and the extreme levels of poverty confronting communities, young girls are persuaded into marriage, which comes along with sexual, physical, and emotional abuse. Apio, a 16-year-old fourth wife and mother of one helps to substantiate this point:

> When we came back (from the camp), we had nothing. Not even food. My mother offered me out for marriage in return for bride price… the man (her husband) has other wives who hate me because I am younger. They give me a lot of work; they say demeaning statements before our husband, such as I being a bad cook.

This quote has significant messages from both feminist and indigenous epistemologies. The quote above elaborates the local indigenous understanding relating to bride price as significant for forging communal relations to obtain security. In-laws broaden the social network; affirm a sense of belonging and also ensure access to resources including land. Marriage is thus a necessity for survival. Apio is disadvantaged in this marriage not only because of her age, but also due to her status as the fourth wife with one child. According to African indigenous feminist thought, the group has priority over the individual, even though the individual is appreciated within the group (Chilisa 2012). In northern Uganda, the younger generation is socialized to respect elders (including co-wives). If Apio is to pass for a good wife to the husband, other women and the community must also accept her. Even though the war has undermined adult influence, elders still largely oversee the institution of marriage. Childbirth also is about labor, as women are expected to fulfill their domestic chores with the help of their children. Having one small child means that Apio must do all the chores by herself. Workload according to this marriage is shared among women on scheduled days. Apio therefore is expected to perform her roles just like other women with more children do on their stipulated days. This arrangement though unfair to Apio, is a culturally expected way for individual women to demonstrate their abilities in a polygamous marriage. Had Apio been the first wife, irrespective of her age she would enjoy a different kind of status that would put her in a relatively privileged position. This case clearly elaborates how multiple identities can intersect to perpetuate various forms of violence against particular groups, in this case, young women. Here, Apio is disadvantaged by her age (16), marital status (4th wife), and number of children (1), as well as being in an inevitable marriage due to poverty in a war-torn area.

When post-conflict reconstruction programs fail to take into consideration culturally and locally relevant contexts and meanings attached to social categories, they overlook the experiences of particular community members like Apio. This is because such individuals are ideally youth but would not identify themselves as such given the people they relate with and the roles they perform in society. Apio specifically relates with other wives, and performs the roles of a mother and wife, all of which qualify her as an adult. Individuals like Apio exclude themselves from youth activities as a way of respecting communal notions pertaining to their identities. Programs targeting youth, therefore, need to appreciate and include communal understandings, beliefs, and perceptions if all female youth are to benefit from their services.

Drawing on a Black feminist perspective, Apio's case demonstrates how women are complicit to exploitation, marginalization, and subordination to other women due to differences in class and status, but also age. Humanitarian assistance exacerbates this marginalization by solely emphasizing gender as a critical category of analysis, disregarding the specific needs of young women grounded in age and marital status. When the differences are recognized, society categorizes female youth as "young women". This indicates their subordinate position within the category "women" as relatively immature, which in turn marginalizes their participation in decision-making and related womanly roles. The elder women thus take precedence in representing the category "women".

Post-conflict returned communities also use humanitarian assistance as a way of maintaining social order at the expense of the women and youth. Various institutions, including religious and cultural, expect women to accommodate violence in order to maintain harmony in the family and community. Such male-dominated institutions enforce social control over and among women and girls. During conflict and displacement, the cultural and religious moral values were greatly affected and disintegrated largely due to generational gaps created by the displacement (McDonnell and Akallo 2007; Spitzer and Twikirize 2013). Some aspects, however, remained intact; for instance, all clan leaders are men because culturally women cannot head clans. Besides gendered limitations, in the return areas, there is a clash of ideologies among the older and the younger generation largely due to differences in life experiences. For instance, the older generation believes in collectivization in rural settings while the young prefer individualism in the urban areas. One key informant explained this dilemma:

> The youth are not interested in agriculture. Yes they do not have the skills but they also do not want to live in the villages. Otherwise, they would learn, life is about learning. They like the towns, the loud music playing all day, the electricity. They want to do business and have money all the time.

If elders continue being the exclusive key voices informing reconstruction processes and programs, youth will continue losing out due to conflict of interests because their concerns are not addressed. Elders wish to return (shape community) to pre-conflict social settings. The youth, on the other hand, have varying perceptions about how the community should accommodate emerging dynamics resulting from the conflict. Evidence exists of prejudicial encounters among various community members largely discrediting the youth. This is especially evident in reproductive health issues including use of contraceptives, which specifically implicates the young women. Restrictions on women's movement and use of contraceptives by husbands as a way of maintaining order in their households is also perpetuated by societal structures and institutions such as health centers. Women for instance are skeptical of buying contraceptives since some health workers pass on the information to their husbands, resulting in domestic violence in most cases. They, thus make use of the few women who have permission from husbands and mothers-in-law to use contraceptives to buy the tablets on others' behalf. This can result in serious medical consequences since such women do not go through the required medical examinations, nor receive counseling prior to use of such contraceptives about side effects and when to seek medical help. Prescriptions are made based on the health situation and history of the women that have permission to use such contraceptives. In these cases the health centers require husbands' permission. Community members in their various capacities as health workers, school administrators, and so on, hence create a form of social surveillance, which perpetuates male dominance and control resulting in violence against women and girls. One female respondent noted,

> Some reproductive health centers require that men accept our use of family planning [contraceptives], which is not easy… it is however, also not easy to deal with [secretive use of contraceptives] because if you do not have babies the man can find another woman.

By implementing aid through culturally grounded institutions, humanitarian assistances sustain violence by denying women control over their bodies, time use, and movement. Generally, contraceptive use is culturally discouraged due to misinformation and negative connotations attached to it (Asiimwe et al. 2014), the central one being that women who use it are unfaithful. Contraceptive access and use by youth is even more stigmatized and pathologized by families, cultural elders, and community including health workers and religious leaders. Even within marriage unions, contraceptive use is highly condemned, resulting in women delivering many children. One respondent noted,

> I am married. I and some other married women secretly use family planning. Our husbands do not know because, we do not tell them, as they do not like it. They think (by using birth controls), we want/intend to sleep around with other men, sure of no conception. We discuss with other women on our way to the water wells about available tablets (the most widely used method). We cannot go to health centers because you need permission [from husbands], and if you are not sick, why would you go to the health center?

In addition to birth control, humanitarian assistance provided in the form of antenatal and postnatal care, further marginalizes female youth. First, health workers encourage and at times require women (when major decisions are to be made including use of contraceptives) to obtain those services in the presence of their husbands. While this is a government idea nationally as a way of encouraging male involvement in women's reproductive health, humanitarian agencies tag assistance in the form of "food for health" to fulfill health center requirements. This ended up negatively impacting some individuals, especially the young women. In post-conflict settings like northern Uganda some girls are raped (Porter 2013), others have multiple partners as a survival strategy, and still others are involved in prostitution—where clients pay more money for live sex (Bricker 2009). Therefore, demanding a pregnant woman to go with her husband or partner indicates a norm that presupposes marriage before sex and/or pregnancy. For fear of humiliation and stigmatization from the medical practitioners, girls choose not to participate in tagged humanitarian services. Girls noted that health centers staff display negative attitudes toward contraceptive use by youth and especially unmarried young women.

Stigma connected to and criminalization of reproductive practices discourages young women from using such services yet young people do not have a practical way to effectively manage sexual activeness. Contraceptive use is not supported socially and culturally. Abortion, on the other hand, is a criminal offence in Uganda. It cannot therefore be administered under professional medical supervision. Despite its criminalization, abortion is still carried out illegally using unsafe abortion methods such as local herbs and detergent soap (Omo and Nomi). Such substances are used because they are readily and cheaply available. These, however, have serious health effects including internal damage and severe bleeding. Besides health repercussions, abortion is culturally and religiously stigmatized and often results in isolation of the women and girls when identified. The fear for stigmatization hinders women who experience unsuccessful abortions from accessing medical centers even though post-abortion care is provided in government hospitals and health centers. A medical worker in a previous study, for instance, noted that girls went to seek medical help only in extreme cases of unsuccessful abortions including serious abnormal pain and excessive bleeding (Namuggala 2010). One female highlighted the silence around the practice:

> We cannot talk about it (abortion); people think you are a prostitute and a murderer, a traitor who does not support the rebuilding of the community. Even when you don't do it, simply talking about it is enough for people around you to conclude that you are morally unfit for the community.

The criminalization of abortion also results in self-policing among women and girls. Due to policing relating to contraceptive use and abortion, girls and women in most cases are forced to carry unwanted pregnancies including those resulting from rape. In this case, the government of Uganda, by illegalizing and criminalizing abortion is complicit with patriarchal cultural frameworks to indirectly propagate sexual violence against women and girls. Humanitarian assistance contributes to this violence in two ways. First by working through government health centers, it hinders women's participation. Second humanitarian assistance, in the form of "food for health" that caters mainly for expectant and nursing mothers, is meant to encourage motherhood but not necessarily foster women and girls' individual decisions to be mothers. Aid for instance should also be tagged to post-abortion care as a way of encouraging women to go for post medical care after termination of pregnancies.

Another institution that has sustained violence against young women is the school. Humanitarian assistance provided in schools in the form of "food for education" and scholastic materials, is reliant on regular attendance of schools including timely arrival (8.00 a.m.) when the class roll call/register is taken and late departures when schools close. Given the gender division of labor, girls have domestic chores to complete before going to school and thus report late. The portion of food received by the schools is therefore reduced since teachers mark absenteeism when students reported late. Participants also reported stigmatization in schools, where girls who are identified as having been pregnant or having aborted are dismissed from school irrespective of the circumstances surrounding the pregnancy or abortion. Given the negative portrayals such girls encounter, rejoining school after childbirth is very difficult. A quick comparison with boys, however, indicates that even when they are responsible for the pregnancies, they continue with their education without any interruption. This demonstrates how female youth are disproportionately marginalized in access to and use of resources and services provided in northern Uganda's post-conflict reconstruction phase.

During the study, participants mentioned that dismissal of pregnant girls was done because schools have to maintain a good reputation in the community by eliminating "bad girls" or else it would become common practice for girls to "misbehave" by being sexually active. This attitude is not unique to northern Uganda but rather a nationwide concern. Ahikire and Madanda (2011) highlight the lack of clear policies about how schools should handle pregnancies. There is a dearth of information on dropouts due to pregnancy and whether they rejoin school or not. There is a lack of a comprehensive framework to address cases of pregnancies in schools. Consequently, schools adopt various measures including expulsion.

Communally, the girls are rejected and at times sent away from their families as outcasts (Ahikire and Madanda 2011). Education is a fundamental human right emphasized in the 1995 Uganda constitution and also in the United Nations Convention on the Rights of the Child to which Uganda is signatory. Despite these instruments, girls who fall pregnant are structurally denied the chance to enjoy this right. Schools, community, and even families in northern Uganda turn against the girls since they are expected to be sexually inactive until marriage.

More to that, humanitarian assistance is framed with certain messages that challenge its principle of neutrality. According to the United States Department of State (2010), an estimated 85% of the Ugandan population is Christian. In a majority Christian nation, Christian organizations have been active in post-conflict phase providing aid, but that the message of abstinence and abortion as sin especially harms young women. Religious teachings function to pathologize and discourage abortion and other practices including condom use, especially among the unmarried young population. Christians in Uganda restrict sexual freedom especially sex before and outside marriage among other moral attributes. Christian groups, while not formally recognized as humanitarian oriented, are very active in the post-conflict phase providing material as well as psychological aid in form of counseling, encouraging forgiveness and reconciliation and preaching to the communities. Most important for this study is that these fail to acknowledge the fact that youth are sexually active. Emphasis is put on abstinence till marriage. While abstinence is the recommended avenue to guard against unwanted pregnancies, HIV, and other Sexually Transmitted Infections (STIs), it is clear that it is practically very difficult for most youth especially those in war-torn regions like northern Uganda where children in camps were exposed to sex early, and others were raped (Gates and Reich 2010). Preaching against abortion as sin, however, puts female youth in a double bind, with no easy way out. The practical realities they encounter tend to conflict with the spiritual and moral guidance into which they have been or are being socialized. This denies youth any control over their bodies and sexual rights, which perpetuates marginalization. The preaching, therefore, needs to be applied to the experiences young women encounter in order to deal with the practical issues they face. Being idealistic does not seem to provide a lasting solution to especially female youth-related challenges.

As the preceding discussion demonstrates, humanitarian assistance provision has facilitated violence, discrimination, and marginalization against young women through the institutions in private and public spaces including schools, streets and homes, as well as political, economic, social, and legal institutions (Barak 2003; Dolan 2009). While the returned population is seriously challenged by the assistance, humanitarian agencies also face a number of challenges, which affect the operations of their services and programs.

Conclusion

This chapter has argued that single categorical analysis based on gender or age misrepresents the experiences of female youth who simultaneously occupy these multiple categories. Single level analysis while dealing with humanitarian recovery assistance is not sufficient, and results in violence against young women. This is because informal (social, cultural, religious), and formal (humanitarian and government) structures work hand in hand to marginalize women and girls. It is important to come up with holistic approaches to ensure that humanitarian programs do not entrench patriarchal dominance that harms women in recovery assistance programs in northern Uganda. This demands consideration of institutional and structural violence while acknowledging the interconnections and overlaps such violence has with interpersonal and individual violence.

Finally, listening to the voices of the most marginalized and focusing on them is a crucial component in postwar reconstruction. As Alcoff (2008) contends, the problems of speaking for others include misrepresentation, marginalization, and exclusion that may ultimately undermine the very assistance humanitarian agencies seek to provide. While the armed violence by the Lord's Resistance Army has been a major contributor, the humanitarian crisis in northern Uganda is also informed by other factors including drought, floods, historical marginalization, poor infrastructure, and diseases. All these factors must be considered if communities are to attain self-sustenance.

Despite the challenges that confront humanitarian assistance, this assistance nonetheless has played a great role in responding to the mandate of ending human suffering in northern Uganda by providing basic needs like food and medical care. Due to limited intersectional analysis relating to gender, age, parenthood, and marital status, however, it has perpetuated violence especially against women and girls in the form of sexual harassment, physical abuse and psychological torture as discussed above. This, demands immediate attention. While communities face challenges, implementing agencies also have constraints involving natural disasters and insecurity within the region, administrative hindrances involving funders' unrealistic conditions as well as corruption especially from the government officials. Improving the conditions of formerly displaced communities in northern Uganda necessitates a holistic approach that brings together the various stakeholders involved including donors, government (structures and institutions), nongovernmental agencies, cultural, and religious leaders as well as the returning communities to map out circumstances and lay strategies. Stakeholders need to speak to each other if sustainable return and resettlement is to be attained in northern Uganda.

Given the preceding discussion, I call for the implementation of programs to recognize and address the diversity of experiences within the category "women" in order to achieve more equitable societies in the aftermath of conflict. An intersectional approach that examines other factors that inform intra-group gender relations including age, motherhood and marital status is therefore necessary for a peaceful and sustainable post-conflict reconstruction.

References

Ahikire, J., & Madanda, A. (2011). *A report on re-entry of pregnant girls in primary and secondary schools in uganda*. FAWE Uganda. http://www.education.go.ug/files/downloads/gender_Report%20on%20Girls%20Re-ntry%20in%20school.pdf.

Alcoff, L. (2008). The problem of speaking for others. In A. Jaggar (Ed.), *Just methods: An interdisciplinary feminsit reader* (pp. 145–171). London: Paradiagm Publishers.

Annan, J., Blattman, C., Mazurana, D., & Carlson, K. (2011). Civil war, reintegration, and gender in northern Uganda. *Journal of Conflict Resolution*, 55(6), 877–908.

Asiimwe, J. B., Ndugga, P., Mushomi, J., & Ntozi, J. P. (2014). *Factors associated with modern contraceptive use among young and older women in Uganda: A comparative analysis*. http://bmcpublichealth.biomedcentral.com/articles/10.1186/1471-2458-14-926.

Barak, G. (2003). *Violence and nonviolence: Pathways to understanding*. London: Sage.

Branch, A. (2007). Uganda's civil war and the politics of ICC intervention. *Ethics & International Affairs*, 21(2), 179–198.

Bricker, M. (2009). Girl soldiers: The cost of survival in northern Uganda. Women News Network. *Alternet*.

CEDOVIP. (2016). *Domestic violence act coalition advocacy pays off: Cabinet approves the national gender based violence policy 2016*. http://www.cedovip.org/index.php/resources/publications/other-publications/54-article-gbv-policy-final/file.

Chai, J., Fink, G., Kaaya, S., Danaei, G., Fawzi, W., Ezzati, M., et al. (2016). Association between intimate partner violence and poor child growth: Results from 42 demographic and health surveys. *Bulletin of the World Health Organization, 94*, 331–339. https://doi.org/10.2471/BLT.15.152462.

Cheney, K. (2007). *Pillars of the nation: Child citizens and Ugandan national development*. Chicago and London: The University of Chicago Press.

Chilisa, B. (2012). *Indigenous research methodologies*. London: Sage.

Christie, D. J., Wagner, R. V., & Winter A. D. (Eds.). (2001). *Peace, conflict and violence: Peace psychology for the 21st century*. Engelwood Cliffs, NJ: Prentice-Hall.

Dolan, C. (2002). Collapsing masculinities and weak states—A case study of northern Uganda. In F. Cleaver (Ed.), *Masculinities matter! Men, gender, and development* (pp. 57–84). New York: Zed Books.

Dolan, C. (2009). *Social torture: The case of northern Uganda, 1986–2006*. New York and Oxford: Berghahn Books.

Dolan, C., & Hovil, L. (2006). *Humanitarian protection in Uganda. A trojan horse?* (HPG Background Paper 30). London: Oversees Development Institute.

Emergency, Response and Recovery. (2010). *Guidance emergency, response and recovery*. UK Cabinet Office. https://www.gov.uk/government/publications/emergency-response-and-recovery.

Galtung, J. (1969). Violence, peace and peace research. *Journal of Peace Research, 6*(3), 167–191.

Gates, S., & Reich, S. (Eds.). (2010). *Child soldiers in the age of fractured states*. Pittsburg: University of Pittsburgh Press.

Gelsdorf, K., Maxwell, D., & Mazurana, D. (2002). *Livelihoods, basic services and social protection in northern Uganda and Karamoja*. London: Feinstein International Center.

Global Humanitarian Assistance Report. (2016). *Vulnerability, poverty, crisis. Development initiatives*. https://reliefweb.int/sites/reliefweb.int/files/resources/Global-Humanitarian-Assistance-Report-2016.pdf.

Harrell-Bond, B. (1986). *Imposing aid: Emergency assistance to refugees*. Oxford: Oxford University Press.

Human Rights Watch. (2005). *Uprooted and forgotten: Impunity and human rights abuses in northern Uganda*. New York: Human Rights Organization.

IDMC. (2008). *Uganda: Focus shifts to securing durable solutions for IDPS*. Geneva: Internal Displacement Monitoring Center.

International Organization for Migration. (2012). *International dialogue on migration: Protecting migrants during times of crisis: Immediate responses and sustainable strategies (21)*. Geneva: International Organization for Migration.

Jones-Casey, K., Dick, L., & Bizoza, A. (2014). *The gendered nature of land and property rights in post-reform Rwanda*. Kigali and Rwanda: USAID | LAND Project.

Kalin, W., Williams, R., Koser, K., & Solomon, A. (2010). *Incorporating the guiding principles on internal displacement into domestic law: Issues and challenges* (Studies in Transnational Legal Policy No. 41). Washington: The American Society of International Law, Brookings.

Kerker, B. D., Zhang, J., Nadeem, E., Stein, R. E. K., Hurlburt, M. S., Heneghan, A., et al. (2015). Adverse childhood experiences and mental health, chronic medical conditions, and development in young children. *Academic Pediatrics, 15,* 510–517. https://doi.org/10.1016/j.acap.2015.05.005.

Kindi, F. I. (2010). *Challenges and opportunities for women's land rights in the post-conflict northern Uganda* (MICROCON Research Working Paper No. 26). Brighton: MICROCON. Retrieved September 9, 2015 from http://www.microconflict.eu/publications/RWP26_KFI.pdf.

March, C., Smyth, I., & Mukhopadhy, M. (1999). *A guide to gender-analysis frameworks*. Oxford: Oxfam.

McDonnell, F., & Akallo, G. (2007). *Why it matters and what you can do: Girl soldiers: A story of hope for northern Uganda's children*. Grand Rapids, MI: Chosen Books Publishers.

McKay, S. (2004). Reconstructing fragile lives: Girls' social reintegration in northern Uganda and Sierra Leone. *Gender & Development, 12*(3), 19–30.

McKay, S., & Mazurana, D. (2004). *Where are the girls? Girls in fighting forces in northern Uganda, Sierra Leone, and Mozambique: Their lives during and after the war*. Quebec, CA: Rights and Democracy.

Menjívar, C. (2011). *Enduring violence: Ladina women's lives in Guatemala*. London: University of California Press.

Moortz, J., Stabble, S., & Mollen, D. (2017). Gender based violence and armed conflict: A community informed socio ecological conceptual model from northern Uganda. *Psychology of Women Quarterly, 41*(3), 368–388.

Namuggala, V. F. (2010). *Gender analysis of humanitarian assistance programs in post conflict northern Uganda: The case of food and reproductive health in Lira district*. MA thesis, unpublished Makerere University, Kampala.

Namulondo, S. (2012, December 11, Tuesday). *Uganda police named most corrupt institution*. http://www.independent.co.ug/news/news/7025-uganda-police-named-most-corrupt-institution.

O'Callaghan, S., & Gilbride, K. (2008). *From the grass-roots to the security council: Oxfam's humanitarian advocacy in Darfur*. The Democratic Republic of Congo and Uganda, Humanitarian Policy Group Overseas Development Institute, London.

OCHA. (2011, November 20). *OCHA on message: Humanitarian principles.* Retrieved on http://www.unocha.org/about-us/publications/humanitarian-principles.
Ochen, E. A., Jones, A. D., & McAuley, J. W. (2012). Formerly abducted child mothers in northern Uganda: A critique of modern structures for child protection and reintegration. *Journal of Community Practice, 20*(1–2), 89–111.
Office of the Prime Minister (OPM). (2007, September). *Peace, recovery and development plan for northern Uganda (PRDP) 2007–2010.* Kampala: Government of Uganda.
Porter, H. (2013). *After rape: Justice and social harmony in northern Uganda.* Ph.D. thesis, The London School of Economics and Political Science (LSE).
Refugee Documentation Center. (2010). *Are there reports of sexual violence against women and girl children in Uganda?* Refugee Documentation Centre of Ireland on 16 June 2010.
Relief Web. (2008). *Glossary of humanitarian terms.* http://www.who.int/hac/about/reliefweb-aug2008.pdf?ua=1.
Sjoberg, L. (2013). *Gendering global conflict: Toward a feminist theory of war.* New York: Columbia University Press.
Smith, L. T. (2012). *Decolonizing methodologies: Research and indigenous peoples.* London: Zed Books.
Soto, R. (2009). *Tall grass: Stories of suffering and peace in northern Uganda.* East Lansing: Michigan State University Press.
Spitzer, H., & Twikirize, J. (2013). War affected children in northern Uganda: No easy path to normality. *International Social Work, 56,* 67–79.
Tim, A., & Vlassenroot, K. (2010). *The lord's resistance army: Myth and reality.* London: Zed Books.
Tripp, A. (2004). Women's movement, customary law and land rights in Africa: The case of Uganda. *African Studies Quarterly, 7*(4), 1–19.
United States Department of State. (2010, November 17). *Report on international religious freedom—Uganda.* Retrieved January 8, 2016, from http://www.refworld.org/docid/4cf2d05b82.html.
Wane, N. N. (2003). Embu women: Food production and traditional knowledges, resources for feminist research. *FRF Journal Volume, 30*(1/2), 137–148.
World Health Organization. (2013). *Global and regional estimates of violence against women: Prevalence and health effects of intimate partner violence and non-partner sexual violence.* Retrieved from http://apps.who.int/iris/bitstream/10665/85239/1/9789241564625_eng.pdf.
World Vision International. (2017). *World Vision President Kevin Jenkins visits refugee response in northern Uganda.* Retrieved from https://www.wvi.org/africa/article/world-vision-president-kevin-jenkins-visits-refugee-response-northern-uganda.

CHAPTER 7

Young People's Agency and Resilience

INTRODUCTION

This chapter focuses on the agency and resilience of young people during the conflict and in post-conflict situations. The chapter highlights that children are not entirely victims and vulnerable but rather resilient and creative. To bring out their agentic nature, I discuss the coping strategies young people adopted during challenging situations during and after forced displacement, i.e. in abduction, encampment and in return areas. I explore the capabilities young people in northern Uganda demonstrate in sustaining livelihoods and survival. In discussing agency, I go beyond the impact of the civil war to include other challenges the region is undergoing. Besides war and displacement, northern Uganda has encountered many problems including absolute poverty largely explained by unbalanced regional development, food insecurity due to natural disasters like drought and floods, cattle rustling especially from the neighboring Karimajong cattle rustlers, and outbreaks of diseases. Resilience thus reflects young people's agency in all these situations. It is important to understand and acknowledge how young people have managed to survive through these complex multidimensional challenges by exploring the choices and decisions they make. For instance, I explain why some members chose to stay in the camps despite official closure and what impact this had on their lives. This is one way of decolonizing the

© The Author(s) 2018
V. F. Namuggala, *Childhood, Youth Identity, and Violence in Formerly Displaced Communities in Uganda*, Critical Cultural Studies of Childhood, https://doi.org/10.1007/978-3-319-96628-1_7

conventional understanding of young people's identity in war as entirely victims and thus vulnerable in need of protection from adults.

For a better appreciation of children's resilience especially in responding to the effects of conflict, I explain the conditions that result in the use of certain resilience strategies and give a context-specific understanding of agency and resilience. This is followed by a brief overview of children's experiences during conflict and post-conflict phases. This sets the foundation for the mechanisms young people to apply as a way of survival in which I provide a detailed examination of the strategies they organize.

Contextualizing Resilience and Agency

This volume adopts the understanding of resilience as "the capacity of communities in complex socio-ecological systems to learn, cope, adapt and transform in the face of shocks and stresses" (Corps 2015: 7). Specifically, this chapter concentrates on how children and youth in conflict-affected situations adapt to changing socioeconomic situations, and transform their identity and perceptions in order to survive under the changing circumstances during displacement, encampment, and return. Resilience specifically involves how young people make and maintain important connections, networks, and relationships between themselves and with other people in the community. I, in addition, analyze the strategies they adapt to engage systems and structures creating and sustaining their vulnerabilities.

Agency, on the other hand, is conceptualized as a provisional process of social engagement which is informed by the past, oriented toward the future, and rooted in the present circumstances (Emirbayer and Mische 1998). This chapter thus conceptualizes agency as a continual process involving individuals and groups at varying levels. I examine how children and youth evaluate and reconstruct the conditions they experience in the post-conflict phase while they look back to their pre-conflict and during conflict experiences. I link post-conflict experiences to the historical experiences of the region (including armed conflict and colonialism) while analyzing the impact they have for the future. I examine the various forms of oppression, the power relations embedded within them, and the simultaneous subordination of young people in the social, political, and economic structures. I emphasize how young people as individuals and in groups intentionally determine their actions depending on available resources to achieve their desired goals.

Unlike refugees (who are displaced outside their home countries and are a responsibility of the United Nations High Commissioner for Refugees) (UNHCR), the IDPs pause a complex situation. They are legally still under the protection and care of their home governments, which at times have contributed to their predicament, for instance, in the case of northern Uganda. The guiding principles on internal displacement are encouraged to guide how to deal with situations of internal displacement. These are however, not legally binding to any stakeholders. As such nation state governments cannot be held accountable for their actions or failure to act in relation to IDPs. Scholars consequently observe that internal displacement is a war crime and a crime against humanity to which no one is held accountable (Branch 2007) despite the world having 38 million internally displaced persons (IDMC 2015).

The years dominated by the civil war had profound impacts on communities in northern Uganda. The impacts, however, had gendered and age differentials in experience. For instance, the war affected women's self- perceptions, yet at the same time impacted men's perceptions of women in northern Uganda. It has also to be noted that women and children returning from armed groups were able to reintegrate socially and were more psychologically resilient compared to men (Annan et al. 2011). This, however, does not mean women and children faced lesser challenges (Soto 2009). It is their resilience and agency that aids such reconstruction. The following section examines children and youth's experiences and strategies adopted during the conflict.

Young Peoples' Experiences and Strategies During Displacement

Displacement in this volume specifically refers to experiences both in the battlefield—"the bush" and encampment. I refer to study participants who lived with the rebels as having lived in the bush, while those who lived in internally displaced people's (IDP) camps as encamped. In the previous chapters I have discussed more of the experiences in encampment and here I will focus more on the experiences of those who lived in the bush. The national army controlled the IDP camps while the Lord's Resistance Army rebel forces controlled the bush.

Participants explained that "the bush" was a metaphoric concept that meant, "Where the rebels lived". This was not a permanent physical area of residence but shifted from time to time. One participant, for instance, explained that when the rebels attacked, the villages (residential areas) became the bush and all civilians were expected to vacate such areas. Importantly, communities had to come up with strategies to avoid the bush. Most participants vividly recalled the night shifts, commonly referred to by scholars as "night commuting"/"night commuters". One contributor elaborated that,

> In the night, the villages became the bushes; we ceased sleeping in our houses unless you were ready to be abducted. We moved from villages at around 5 pm, before it got dark and walked to town centers, churches and other public spaces, even streets to avoid abductions. The rebels normally attacked in the night. We would return in the mornings to farm, plant and harvest.

Another confirmed, "Everyone moved—children, young adults, women and men. We all moved. If you feared for your life you moved". In the evenings, families would vacate their houses for town centers, which were perceived to be safer and more protected, compared to the villages. Carrying their bedding, food, and other basic needs for the night, masses would trek out only to return late morning when the rebels were believed to have returned to the bush.

While civilians developed survival mechanisms during the insurgence, those who were taken by the rebels (referred to henceforth as abductees) improvised differently. Over the duration of the war, the LRA rebels attacked villages in northern Uganda to loot food and animals but also to abduct people as "recruits" for the fighting forces but also as cooks, servants, and wives. These included able-bodied men, women, and children but mainly youth who were considered more energetic. Abductees were restricted in movement and association, and lived under close supervision until they attainted the trust of the rebel leaders. Any signs of mistrust from the rebel leaders resulted in the murder of the abductee(s). One former abductee explained that pretense was the most commonly used survival strategy. She elaborated how no one was sincere in the bush. This was because abductees strived to portray loyalty to and acceptance of the beliefs of the rebels. Irrespective of the methods of conscription, survival demanded a public display of voluntary obedience to everything the leaders required, including indoctrination of newcomers. One participant recounted,

> We even said wrong and bad things about our communities to the rebels, all in the name of winning their [rebel leaders] favor, to show that we had really crossed over to their side. We really pretended a lot. Even when you planned to escape the following day, you would keep humble and polite.

Escaping was one survival strategy that most abductees looked up to in order to return home and have a normal life again. While it was the only way to safety, escaping was risky and dangerous thus so secretively executed. As abductees prepared to escape, another strategy automatically emerged, which was the hiding of food. Returned former abductees explained that if one wanted to survive while on the run, they had to have food to sustain them. The only way to access food during abduction, however, was through the commanders and their wives, which food was limited and thus restricted. For one to have more food for the purpose of keeping it, they had to steal it and hide it. One young woman explained:

> We would hide some of the food from the supervisors. Just in case you have a chance to escape, you have something to feed on. You know, you could not tell how long you would run or keep in hiding. Because you would not even know the route, you would just keep running hoping to get to a town or a home and ask for help.

Participants who were rescued by the Uganda Peoples Defense Forces (UPDF) through ambushes on the rebel camps didn't have to go through this but rather had to demonstrate to the army that they were abducted and not part of the rebel groups. These had to give out information relating to rebels and demonstrate to the army their urge to return home.

Change of names was a very important strategy used both in the bush and return areas. Informants explained that to change one's name helped to forget past memories and create a new sense of identity thereby facilitating reintegration, remembering, and resettlement. One young woman said, "*When people don't call you by the name under which you killed or suffered, then you can forget as time passes by. You start being a normal human being again*". They further explained further that when stigmatized and rejected by their communities, girls would move to other areas where they would take on new names to mark a change in their lives. In most instances, girls would take on names that implied the kind of life they wished to live. Some of the names included Peace, Mercy, Charity, and Patience. These names carried a contextually relevant meaning by calling for unity and love among community members. While naming in Uganda is normally gender specific, these names tended to be gender neutral emphasizing the responsibility for all community members to work toward harmony and peace. Proclaiming out loud what they wanted was one way for the participants to get closer to the life they desired. These young people desire a peaceful life where people get along with each other, are patient with one another and are not judgmental, especially to returnees from the bush. These participants had expected return areas to be homes yet they continued to be torture zones due to violence, stigmatization, discrimination, and marginalization. When involved in socially unacceptable activities like prostitution, girls explained that they also used different names to protect their social identity by disguising as different people. Girls embraced their "community names" when they participated in socially acceptable behavior. They thus had two sets of names strategically used according to location and occupation.

While some young women changed names on their own accord, others had no control over their names. The rebels also used name changing as a strategy to control their abductees. Some rebel leaders at times changed the names of abductees as a way of asserting power and erasing memories of family and community by changing who the abductees had previously known themselves to be. One participant explained how she was "re-baptized" with a new name by one of the rebels upon abduction. She said,

> When we were taken, one of the men gave me a name. He re-baptized me. He said your name is Agnes [not real name] and you will be called like that. When others asked for my name as we walked, he would turn and look at me and I would respond, "Agnes". Everyone thought that was my name and all the time in the bush they called me Agnes.

While this naming was against her will and control, it served Agnes well in the post-conflict stage. When I asked whether she changed it when she returned home, Agnes explained, "No, I didn't because people in the village called me by my original name. They didn't know that I was also Agnes (the name given to her by the rebel leader on abduction and she was referred to as such till she escaped). It's like I had two people in me". For her, Agnes remained in the bush while the "original" community member returned to the village. This helped her overcome some of the trauma and accept her new post-conflict life.

Rebel leadership, in addition, rewarded violence, exertion of power and control, especially against women. Rebel forces considered bravery and fierceness as critical qualities for promotion among abductees. Participants mentioned that rebels had something different in relation to seniority and leadership compared to the cultural construction of power and masculinity. While traditionally age (functional and relational) is very important, and men are responsible for protection of and provision for their families, informants highlighted that violence and commitment influenced seniority and authority in the LRA. As such, young men who demonstrated willingness to kill, rape, and burn huts had higher chances of promotion than the older men, many of whom were abducted but did not find pleasure in violence. The rebels termed nonviolence cowardice, a sign of limited commitment to the cause of the rebel group. Power dynamics within the bush largely centered on positioning women as objects on to which men's dominance was manifested. In his discussion of civil war in Sierra Leone, Chris Coulter termed this kind of hierarchical construction "violent meritocracy" (2009: 107) which is common in contemporary rebel/civil war activities. Young men thus survived through violence especially against women.

Tired of constantly being objectified and treated as the other by the fighting forces, some women joined armed forces as a survival strategy. In the armed forces, women worked in various capacities as fighters and spies while others became wives to soldiers. During conflict and especially abduction, securing protection was vital. Protection included security from violent attacks, safety from rape and sexual exploitation, and protection from hunger. One female youth explained,

> Some women joined the army in search for protection. For us who stayed in the camp, safety came with being in the company of armed forces. If men came to learn that you have a relationship with the army men, they would not disturb you much. Having a relationship with man in the army was a source of security for many women. Army men give some money and a sense of security. They protect your family too.

While this reaffirms conventional constructions of the masculine as the protector and feminine as the protected, participants explained that being in the company of the masculine male provided some sense of security. Masculinity was thus crucial for the armed forces, yet it disadvantaged the civilian men. Civilian men during the conflict were emasculated through restricted movement that restrained their ability to protect and provide for their families. Women therefore consciously made the decision to be involved with armed forces and used their bodies as the tool for their own safety as well as the safety of their families.

Some other young women survived by voluntarily submitting to sexual relationships, especially with rebel commanders. This assured them of not only security but also food and other important needs. Young women also tried to demonstrate support and volunteered to do activities that were suitable for women. Such activities included serving as intelligence agents in the form of spies. It also involved mobilization of food, especially in cases where the rebels ran short of food. Young women would also offer drugs to the rebels. They planted marijuana gardens around the houses, which they would sundry and keep in times of plenty and bring it out during times of scarcity. This would give women privileged positions and reduce their susceptibility to sexual and general abuse and violence.

While all the strategies discussed above were important, the study participants generally agreed that in the bush the most crucial strategy was to escape and return home. Yet escape also was the most risky because if one was caught, they were assured of death. Escape, which demanded teamwork was difficult since abductees were suspicious of each other. In trying to win the favor of leaders, some abductees would report colleagues suspected of planning to escape. When one was caught, the respondents explained that they were treated as traitors and spies who were escaping in order to provide information to the government forces. As a way of discouraging others, rebel leaders punished culprits by killing them publically and at times promoting and/or rewarding the person who reported. In addition, the LRA used violence as a way of disempowering older abducted men by having them take orders from young ones. This greatly impacted the conduct of young men in the post-conflict phase because they were used to being rewarded for what the community considered bad behavior. Hence, the violence that has continued especially against women and girls in the form of rape and defilement in return areas is partly associated to experiences of youth during conflict. A detailed examination of post-conflict experiences follows.

Youth Experiences and Strategies in Areas of Return

Prior to conflict, northern Uganda was established as an agriculturally sustained region. Agriculture provided livelihood in the form of food and sale of surplus plant and animal production. Land was communally accessed and used through lineages. This structure was, however, greatly affected by the war and displacement, which turned communities into dependents surviving on food handouts provided through humanitarian assistance. As a way of regaining self-sustenance, the population in northern Uganda returned to agriculture at the end of the conflict. Prior to conflict, northern Uganda had clear distinctions on the gendered division of household labor, especially in relation to production of food and cash crops. Women mainly concentrated on subsistence food production while the men dominated the growing of cash crops, marketing of produce, and trade. This gender structure, however, changed during displacement and shifted the power dynamics in the households. Family survival now became dependent on women. In addition, food crops including millet, maize, groundnuts, cassava and sweet potatoes, and vegetables became income-generating crops. This change blurred the dichotomy between cash crops and food crops hence impacting the gender division of labor in the region.

The shift in crop categorization brought in income. It also, however, negatively affected food security in the household. With food crops now becoming commercial crops, there is no clear-cut line between what is specifically for food and what is for income generation. This resulted in subsequent conflicts between wives and husbands. Women want and try to make decisions on what portion of the crops grown should be reserved for subsistence/home consumption. But because the very same crops can earn cash, men want to dictate what should be sold off in the market. Accordingly, conflicts emerge over rationing of crops grown, as well as over money earned from sale of crops and the limited land on which crops are grown. This has also greatly impacted young people's access to productive land. In explaining the effect of commercial production, one key informant explained that environmental degradation in the form of bush burning was on the rise, and land wrangles escalated as the demand for big chunks of cultivatable land increased.

Commercial farming demands big pieces of land. As men take bigger portions of the available land, women and youth's chances for use of land get slimmer. Given that the land had become bushy, communities use bush burning as a way of clearing the land. This is environmentally not recommended. In addition the practice also destroys unintended plantations.

Commercial farming further intensified women's workload as they produced food crops for sale under the control of men. For women to keep some produce at home, they had to produce more than the usual.

Amidst such challenges, gendered identities emerged as an essential organizing principle that worked along with age and other identifying markers especially marital status and motherhood. Women explained that their individual experiences shared a lot of similarities that they started framing such concerns as women's concerns that necessitated them to come up with strategies to resolve them hence fostering their unity. The coping mechanisms women employed thus varied from individual to group strategies. Individual strategies generally involved the use of the body while group interventions largely used gender-specific group strategies. Young men and women used a number of strategies to challenge adult male domination and in the process demonstrated their capabilities, agency and resilience.

Challenging Victimization

Following a discussion of the experiences above, I wish to emphasize that, children and young people generally in northern Uganda challenge victimization grounded in gender but also age by taking on responsibilities which confront gender and age restrictions. They are agentic and resilient, and devise mechanisms for survival amidst constrained environments. The following section of the chapter centers on young people's agency and resilience in post-conflict northern Uganda.

Displacement hindered civilian men's abilities to provide for and protect their families through confinement that restricted freedom of movement and association with other men. This shifted household headship and important decision-making responsibilities to the women. In the post-conflict, this pattern of male absence from the households has persisted as compared to women's increased participation. Women have attained a new status that they are struggling to maintain as providers and protectors in the post-conflict life. Even in homes where men reside as husbands, women heavily contribute to household survival. Young women, however, are more involved in decision-making than the older women. One respondent explains women's positive attitude to this change,

> When you have a problem, you are forced to think so hard to find a solution or else you die. It is a matter of life and death. This situation [war] changed everything for the worst; it created a problem, which we had to solve by ourselves. New problems need new solutions.

The conservatives and cultural gatekeepers within the community nonetheless do not welcome such "new" solutions. Women's progressive survival strategies including working for pay outside the domestic spaces, competing with men for workspaces and doing work that the community considers inappropriate for instance sex work. Women working outside domestic spaces have encountered resistance especially through limited support from men and conservatives, in most cases older women. Individual women who embrace such changes also confront criticism and pathologization for working to sustain their families. One woman metaphorically stated, "The seeds of the fruit are within the fruit". This meant that it was upon women to realize their abilities within themselves to step up, provide for and defend their families, especially in the absence of men who were culturally responsible for maintenance of the household. Women, therefore, sought to fulfill their traditionally stipulated roles in addition to playing "new roles," especially economic provision and protection, which originally were understood as men's roles. Given changing circumstances, women have resorted to using new strategies, which often are culturally deviant, such as sex work. Women risk life and status for the sake of survival for themselves and their families. Sex work is culturally and religiously despised, stigmatized, and pathologized. Besides the social negative attitude, prostitution is also a crime in Uganda. Women are challenging the social construction that frames sex work as "perverted" by using the income earned to maintain socially important aspects and units like the family.

Besides individual strategies like sex work, women initiated women-specific safe spaces. Women in return areas formed into groups with the objective of improving their living conditions and providing support for each other. Women use such spaces for mutual experience sharing, counseling, and guidance over challenging situations. Women encourage each other to keep strong and resilient within their individual spheres. Group formation has greatly improved women's skills in standing up for what they believed in regarding their survival as well as that of their families. While pre-conflict social networks greatly suffered during the war, some central tenets to culture were retained such as collectivity and gender-based group support. Although women acted and experienced situations individually, they realized their experiences were not unique but rather similar. This recognition allowed them to collectively develop strategies such as women using contraceptives secretly without the permission of their husbands as a way of controlling their sexual rights.

Women-formed groups also initiated mechanisms for pooling their resources together and economically supporting each other free of men's influence and control. One example is the utilization of savings and credit schemes. Women who formed groups normally came from the same village and shared common features including being wives and mothers, as well as being heads of households. Shared experiences, challenges, and aspirations could result in groups of women with a membership ranging from 10 to 20 members. Members would periodically, mostly bi-weekly, pool together an agreed amount of money. The collected amounts of money would be made available to members, who would take loans and pay back with affordable minimum interest. Humanitarian agencies also used such groups as a way of reaching targeted communities with support. That was because such groups were more organized and committed. For example, one key informant working with an NGO humanitarian group mentioned that,

> Tukum women's group is a success story of such a mechanism where women used the group to improve their welfare as women and families. We are taking lessons from this group to sensitize other women. Women have used the money to improve their gardens, start small businesses like stalls in the open market as well as buying bicycles for easy transportation.

Besides seeking permission, transportation mechanisms reduce women's dependency on men; owning a bicycle is a big step for women in northern Uganda. The bicycle is the most used type of transportation in the study area. Bicycles are advantageous because they can go through small paths and reach distant areas where open roads do not. Bicycles require no fuel/gas and thus more sustainable for the poor population in the northern Uganda area. A woman who owns a bicycle helps with transporting produce to the market, taking children to health centers and is able to attend meetings in distant locations in time.

Groups thus built an alternative complementary option for identity, sense of belonging and support, and a safety net from abuse from the mainstream social organizing frameworks including the family and religion, which are largely male-dominated. To outsiders, women's groups discuss general concerns such as farming improvement techniques, land management, storage and marketing of produce and child protection and development. To the insiders, however, these groups also deal with women-specific concerns like childbirth control. Such framing of groups was strategic in limiting male intervention and resistance.

Creating group identities also challenges the labeling and blaming of specific individual women. Women noted that working in groups minimized husbands, families, and general communities blaming individual women. One woman said,

> When you are alone, your husband is suspicious that you can be cheating. Even family members start giving you funny looks as if you are doing something fishy. You know how someone looks at you; they don't say anything but then sarcastically smile? That's how it is. But if you are in a group of other women, no one questions.

Groups were therefore crucial for the reintegration of women. They are empowering to individual women by challenging obstacles faced individually through providing collective responsibility. The collective power of the group provided a ground for women to access and utilizes individual rights and freedoms.

Women also organized and forged a group identity that guaranteed them financial independence. Groups broke the collateral barriers that were a hindrance to accessing credit from formal institutions including banks. Despite being largely self-initiated, group formation became a prerequisite for aid by implementing agencies to offer financial aid. Many of the recovery reconstruction agencies, government programs, and Civil Society Organizations acknowledged the power of collectivization. Consequently, they required returned communities to belong to groups as a precondition for accessing services provided in the form of cash loans, farm inputs, and/or trainings. Grouping made accessing, and supervising of communities easier for the humanitarian programs. This approach was highly productive for women, most of whom lacked collateral to acquire loans in traditional financial institutions like banks. Working in groups provided access to such services since group members served as collateral security for each other.

Group formation and participation, however, created some challenges. In a bid to benefit from several different assistance programs, women often belonged to multiple groups simultaneously. Yet, the organizations supporting the various groups had different demands for group members. This constrained women financially as they had to contribute to various groups weekly. Women also allocated a lot of time to be able to participate in the different group meetings. Scholars have termed such participation as "over participation" or "burden of participation" (Ahikire et al. 2012: 45). Scholars have also argued that the single most important gender-related challenge in northern Uganda reconstruction is overwhelming responsibilities placed upon the women (Ahikire et al. 2012). This is complicated because women have placed this responsibility burden on themselves in the need to meet family needs through fulfilling humanitarian assistance demands. Women are creating a bridge between the family and public and thus absorb all the constraints.

While some women complained about over participation, others lamented the exclusions engulfed in the process of group formation. Not everyone could belong to a group given their past experiences and lived realities. Groups also had membership number limitations (at most 20 members), and the formation of new groups required skills including management and accounting that many women did not possess. Second, women's participation was affected by their marital status. Single and widowed women participated more and took decisions without any prior consultations with men, compared to married women who were under the control of men (their husbands) and their in-laws and therefore had to seek their approval before making decisions. Due to inclusion and participation hindrances, even the women's groups marginalized some particular women including sex workers and single mothers, majority of who were young women. Such individuals resorted to other survival mechanisms including relocation.

Some participants considered relocation as a way of dealing with stigmatization and mistreatment by family and general community. Shifting residence to new communities that had less information about one's particular past experiences (for instance, former child soldiers, abductees, and prostitutes) enabled them to be accommodated and forge a sense of community membership. While they acknowledged the challenges of joining a new community without social networks, it was worth trying rather than living in constant torture, blame, and judgment. Relocation allowed change of physical location, getting rid of the negative labeled identity, and letting go of past experiences that held certain individuals captive. Relocation in addition also applied to situations where one left sites of active violence. Informants, however, clarified that although relocation reduces confrontation, it does not mean giving up on what one believes. One participant elaborated,

> I walk away to avoid causing a scene and also show respect to the person accusing me. Since I was a soldier, people in the community think we 'bush children' cannot control anger and violence. The people witnessing will know I did not have a problem but if we both shout, then as a woman I lose. I will walk away but continue doing what I believe I need to do to survive.

Walking away works hand in hand with strategic silence. Feminist scholars have elaborated silence as a form of resistance and empowerment for the marginalized groups. Feminisms nonetheless note that silence is not homogenous since it takes various forms, some of which are victimizing. Applicable in explaining strategic silence is what scholars refer to as "engaged silence" (Rowe and Sheena 2013). Engaged silence is a skill that subordinate groups learn to deliberately control their thoughts and desires. The marginalized consider such thoughts problematic and silencing such voice is emancipating. This is what the participants explained as a strategy they adopted with their colleagues. According to study participants, silence means being able to control one's tongue which permits reflection and allows healing. A formerly abducted child noted that even when insulted, silently "walking away helps you to overcome past negative memories and current outrageous expectations... then when you are alone you can cry". Past memories of the former soldiers mainly involved use of violence in resolving conflicts. Communities continue holding expectations of violence and anger from returned child soldiers, which expectations children fight to break. Other scholars have also noted that generally, society expects former child soldiers to be rude and disrespectful as well as hot-tempered (Lombard and Twikirize 2014). From the perspective of the former soldiers, being able to overcome such expectations of being violent is a big step toward being accepted into the community as "normal" people.

Both silence and "walking away" are, however, context specific. As African indigenous epistemologies clarify, the position of the elders is highly respected. In northern Uganda, youth are socially not expected to talk back but rather be silent before elders unless asked to speak. Silence before elders is thus not a sign of empowerment but rather subordination. Feminist scholars termed this "enforced silence", which complies with hegemonic power structures (Carrillo and Malhotra 2013). In northern Uganda the young generation is compelled to keep silent and to not talk back to elders. In addition, one is not expected to walk away when elders are speaking, and when this happens punishment may be expected. The context under which silence and walking away are used determines whether these actions connote agency or vulnerability. Where youth initiate the silence they are acting as agentic beings but where social construction does not permit them to talk back then they are vulnerable. Study participants clearly understood the difference and explained how they used silence as an empowering strategy especially with age mates and in situations where they felt they were not obliged to explain anything.

Ignoring and/or adapting to live under precarious conditions provided another strategy for survival largely from a gendered perspective. Simultaneous positions for instance of being an ex-soldier, abductee, and female make girls more vulnerable. Formerly abducted child mothers suffer from gender-based stigmatization for having children that were born in the bush. Because the boys that fathered children do not get to return home with them, the community treats the males with less stigmatization compared to the mothers. Participants noted that child–mother stigmatization is so common that girls learn and get accustomed to it. One returned young mother explains how they cope,

> We [girls] have no alternative but to ignore and think less about the problem. We cannot do anything about it. Being judged and misunderstood hurts and I think would hurt any human being, but you can ignore for your own good. You act like you did not hear what they said. You see them staring at you and murmur! Yet you know you are at the center of their talk about you.

While respondents used ignoring as a strategy, this risks resulting in acceptance and internalization of the mistreatment by particular bodies. Failing to act is in itself an act that continues to negatively impact the marginalized members in the community, and sustains gender and age inequalities in the post-conflict phase.

Another aspect where young women demonstrated agency is in family relations, where they challenge the predetermined privileged male position. Culturally, men are expected to head households and thus make all the important decisions within the family. Women are, however, challenging this social construct by refuting some decisions made by men and heading households. Women have become household heads. In Teso, women take on the role of protecting their families, organizing for food, and protecting their children from rape (Liebling-Kalifani et al. 2008). Refuting men's decisions is thus perceived in two major ways. First, some community members think it is disrespectful and a breach of culturally acceptable norms. Others perceive such women positively and perceive them as empowered to be involved in major decisions affecting livelihood and survival. In whichever understanding women's resistance is framed, men feel obliged to maintain women in their "normal" position. Women's improved situation in the post-conflict situation has not been well received especially by men. Society thus challenges women's relative power and wish to maintain women's pre-conflict social status. One male key informant for instance said,

> Women are empowered; I don't call it that way. They are just unruly and misbehaving. When they treat men as if they are useless! Women think they can survive without men. But in my house, they know I am the head and everyone follows my instructions.

Another respondent said,

> We need to work together as men to restore our society to what it used to be [prior to conflict]. Things need to get back to how we were with our great grandparents. Men for instance know how to lead society and everyone knows that. We shall decampaign women who stand against men in the coming elections.

I observed that several leading community opinion leaders, a majority of whom are men, embraced such patriarchal perspectives. They consequently encouraged and believed in the subordination of wives, creating a system that works against the empowerment of women. Naturalization and acceptance of male-dominance results in the limited representation of women and girls in recovery assistance programs. This can encourage the normalization of oppression by the marginalized and its acceptance as the norm in society. Amidst male-biased institutions, women, and girls are compelled to be submissive. Where they conduct themselves differently, women are labeled rebellious, even when what they are doing benefits the family. Irrespective of how society perceives it, some women have maintained their new post-conflict attained social position. It is conversely true that others give into societal pressure to return to pre-conflict gender expectations.

REFERENCES

Ahikire, J., Madanda, A., & Ampaire, C. (2012). *Post-war economic opportunities in northern Uganda: Implications for women's empowerment and participation*. London: International Alert.

Annan, J., Blattman, C., Mazurana, D., & Carlson, K. (2011). Civil war, reintegration, and gender in northern Uganda. *Journal of Conflict Resolution, 55*(6), 877–908.

Branch, A. (2007). Uganda's civil war and the politics of ICC intervention. *Ethics & International Affairs, 21*(2), 179–198.

Carrillo, R. A., & Malhotra, S. (2013). *Silence, feminism, power: Reflections at the edges of sound*. New York: Palgrave Macmillan.

Coulter, C. (2009). *Bush wives and girl soldiers*. New York: Cornell University Press.

Emirbayer, M., & Mische, A. (1998). What is agency? *American Journal of Sociology, 103*, 962–1023.

IDMC. (2015). *Global overview: People internally displaced by conflict and violence*. Geneva: Norwegian Refugee Council.

Liebling-Kalifani, H., Ojiambo-Ochieng, R., Marshall, A., Were-Oguttu, J., Musisi, S., & Kinyanda, E. (2008). Violence against women in northern Uganda: The neglected health consequences of war. *Journal of International Women's Studies, 9*(3), 174–192.

Lombard, A., & Twikirize, J. (2014). Promoting social and economic equality: Social worker's contribution to social justice and social development in South Africa and Uganda. *International Social Work, 57*(4), 313–325.

Mercy Corps. (2015). *Mercy Corps resilience approach*. https://www.mercycorps.org/sites/default/files/Mercy%20Corps%20Resilience%20Approach_April%202015.pdf.

Sheena, M., & Rowe, A. (2013). *Silence, feminism, power: Reflections at the edges of sound*. London: Palgrave Macmillan.

Soto, R. (2009). *Tall grass: Stories of suffering and peace in northern Uganda*. East Lansing: Michigan State University Press.

CHAPTER 8

Conclusion and Recommendations

In this chapter, I make a general wrap up of the book. I also make recommendations largely grounded on the findings of the study but also linked to previous scholarly literature relating to armed violence. Major themes point to **hope and resilience**-youth in northern Uganda have not lost hope despite being referred to by some scholars as a "lost generation". **Positive drive**-youth can be used as positive drivers for peace and reconstruction. They have suffered violence for much of their life but they are also eager to live in a peaceful society. **Social and cultural dynamics**: these play a critical role in resettlement and reintegration especially of youth known by the community to be former combatants. Cultural norms of forgiveness and reconciliation need to be upheld.

- Individualistic and single categorical approaches have not been successful in integrating returning communities. Holistic approaches need to be adopted to avoid stigmatization.

The preceding discussion has so far examined women's agency, resilience and strategies adopted in both displacement and return areas. With a clear understanding of the historical and current situation in northern Uganda, I now turn to conclusions and recommendations. My aim in this section is to make specific indicators that can guide policy formulation and implementation in reconstruction programs. Specifically, I provide ways on how area-operating programs can work with the local communities to end insecurity and its re-occurrence as well as rebuild communities from effects of past violence. I also highlight areas for further research while linking the study to previous literature relating to armed violence and childhood, and within the epistemologies and theoretical frameworks informing the study.

In this section, I offer conclusions largely based on the discussions in the previous chapters. The recommendations target all stakeholders operating in northern Uganda including the state, humanitarian agencies, religious and cultural leaders, and the general community. As a way of addressing pertinent issues emerging from the study, specific conclusions are followed by recommendations with an overarching aim of how best to encourage stability, development, and sustainability in northern Uganda.

To start with, the northern Uganda situation confirmed that different communities understand violence, childhood, adulthood, and family among other terminologies to mean different things. Constructs like child and family in war situations tend to acquire new meanings that impact functions and expectations. These, if not contextually explained, can lead to wrong interpretations and conclusions resulting in poor policies and programs. Fixed, formalized dominant understandings largely informed by the developed world disregard local narratives and overlook local understandings and the meanings communities make out of their own experiences. It is important that in resettlement programs, the language used by different stakeholders (humanitarian agencies, central, and local governments) reflects both social and cultural understandings of intended recipients. It is also crucial for these stakeholders to form collaborative partnerships with essential partners including traditional and cultural leaders, men and the military. The intention of such partnerships would be for purposes of increasing sensitization and awareness about the impact of gender-based violence not only on women and girls but also the entire community, and the nation at large.

The international community, especially the UN, faces various limitations in relation to the developing world's local experiences. Universalistic frameworks play a positive role in society and cannot be wholly discarded as inapplicable to the marginalized regions of the world. Dominant frameworks avail global guiding standards for development, human rights and holding states accountable to these standards. Nation states, however, have fallen complicit or even worse in failing to cater for the socially and culturally relevant conditions citizens encounter. Worth noting is how nation states adopt and domesticate global standards to reflect local realities. For instance, in Chapter 2, UNCRC (1989) defines a child, "as a person below the age of 18, unless the laws of a particular country set the legal age for adulthood younger". I find the ending clause particularly important yet the nation states rarely adapt it. Uganda in its definition adopts 18 as the absolute age disregarding the regional context-specific conditions children experience, which would cater for conditions of children in war-torn regions like northern Uganda. The state of Uganda has failed to use exceptions to apply global standards to the suitability of Ugandans.

Local understandings, moreover, cannot be homogenized because the cultural context in northern Uganda has altered due to social and economic changes resulting in opposing and contradictory perceptions, a case being collectivization. The differentiated views among the local population are linked to their age, length of stay in displacement, and experiences during displacement. Most of the older generation interviewed in the study expressed a strong commitment to the collective wellbeing of children and the general community, while the younger generation was more individualistic in expressing the need for survival and the provision of labor. The youth demonstrated greater vibrancy when their labor was going to be compensated, especially in the form of cash rather than in-kind assistance that would sustain the community. There was also youth who preferred to reside and work in the town centers while the older generation was more optimistic about the rural agricultural life. To minimize such differences, reconstruction programs need to be specific to the demands of the various groups. Youth programs, for instance, might be located in towns, providing skills for trading, banking, saving, and investment instead of forcing youth to return to the villages.

Besides generational survival differences, local perspectives on how to deal with former child soldiers also differed. Intervention programs catering for former child soldiers received contradictory community responses. Some members felt former child soldiers should be held responsible for their actions and ought not to receive preferential treatment programs in the reconstruction phase. Others believed, however, that such children needed to be resocialized for peaceful resettlement. In such situations, it is necessary that reconstruction programs sensitize local communities on the circumstances under which child soldiers became involved in the war, as well as the experiences they had and how society would benefit from having former soldiers reintegrated.

This might minimize judgment from the community and provide rationale for centering on former child soldiers. I agree with Collier's (2000) observation that policies must be distinctive in order to decrease the risk of conflict re-occurring and to cater for the differentiated consequences and opportunities within, between, and among communities that resulted from conflict.

Another clear conclusion this study makes is that communities in northern Uganda do not feel safe despite the government declaration of a post-conflict setting. The feeling of vulnerability was evident from the beginning of my fieldwork when all the respondents refused to sign the consent forms despite their professed eagerness to participate in the study. They explained that, for their own safety, they were not comfortable signing any documents. Even key informants purposively selected for the offices they held, were reluctant to sign forms. While firearms may be put away, peace has not yet returned to the region and communities continue to live in constant fear and mistrust. This affirms earlier scholars' observations that absence of war does not necessarily mean peace (Butler 2010; Machel 2000; Sjoberg 2014). Dealing with this kind of insecurity demands appreciating local understandings of peace and incorporating such understanding in programs and frameworks offered by the formal structures (government and humanitarian programs). The government emphasized disarmament and demobilization of former combatants to limit access to weaponry and discourage reorganization for violent conflict. The local communities, however, perceived peace in form of sustainable reintegration, which comes through reconciliation and forgiveness. Being able to trust their neighbor, ending sexual violence against women and girls, and access to land are some major concerns raised by respondents. This shows how nonmaterial effects of war can have reintegration and resettlement lasting impacts on particular individuals in the community. In addition to disarmament and demobilization, reconstruction programs need to embrace psychosocial frameworks as a way of improving return and reintegration by budgeting, planning, and having activities specifically targeting psychosocial challenges. Communities need to feel and be safe for constructive resettlement to happen in the region.

Related to the above is the conclusion that respondents dreaded the use of force to end violence and recommended peaceful methods including mediation. To the local community, peace between the rebels and the government could not be attained unless peace was locally established. To attain local peace, respondents encouraged mediation between individuals, families, clans, and later armed forces. Mediation is a preferred strategy because it avoids revenge and encourages parties to let go of past differences, which have haunted the region for decades. Even in cases where punishment was recommended, it was in the form of publically asking for forgiveness from the offended party and promising never to repeat the offensive actions.

Researchers and scholars can play a role in improving humanitarian assistance in return areas by actively listening to and writing the voices of the most marginalized to represent locally based concerns and needs. Researchers and assistance providers can intentionally build relationships and alliances between themselves and communities. Such alliances must involve self-reflexivity especially on the part of privileged stakeholders. This study managed to capture complexities because it adopted a holistic approach that embraced both local and formal perspectives on peace, war, and development. I also acknowledged the community as experts of their knowledge and experiences, from whom I was willing to learn. Acknowledging the role of the local community and complexities within the return areas, humanitarian agencies might favor locally relevant perspectives instead of emphasizing dominant views and frameworks. It is critical that agencies place dominant and marginal frameworks in conversation with each other. Both dominant and alternative frameworks offer advantages, which can be adopted, and negatives that can be improved or dropped. The crucial aspect is how these two understandings together might avoid reproducing power hierarchies and impositions that especially burden the local population. One way this can be done is by involving the local communities in humanitarian policy formulation, implementation, and analysis.

The findings of this study indicate that the "logic of masculine protection" at least in the case of northern Uganda has not resulted in greater protection of women and girls. Instead of the state providing protection, the state army, Uganda Peoples Defense Forces (UPDF) was involved in rape and sexual abuse especially within the IDP camps (also see Dolan 2009; Tim and Vlassenroot 2010). Furthermore, some women in northern Uganda actively participated as soldiers during the war (Bricker 2009). Women's involvement challenges common representations that portray women as entirely vulnerable (Butler 2010; Sjoberg 2014; Soto 2009). Instead of being protected, some women directly participated as protectors for the communities and the nation. Despite women's active participation as protectors, compensation during post-conflict for former fighters was linked to gendered roles and thus biased toward men who socially are believed to have been the active players during the war (Puechguirbal 2012). In this way, the state and its institutions demonstrate their gendered assumptions, confirming arguments of the state as a gendered institution (Dill and Zambrana 2009; Tripp et al. 2013). It is prudent therefore that during post-conflict compensation, the government considers roles performed during conflict without gender biases. In addition, dichotomous categorizations of victim vs. perpetrator on the basis of age were challenged in northern Uganda. Women and young people were simultaneously victims as well as perpetrators of violence.

In post-conflict situations, it is helpful to develop local capacities and initiatives. Local initiatives, for instance "Kachope Mandit", a local conflict resolution initiative in Lango region that involved forgiveness and cleansing, seemed to be more effective since the communities identified with such frameworks (Brainard and Chollet 2007). This may be due to the fact these initiatives were demand-driven by communally identified needs. For instance, women formed groups to handle challenges they experienced and membership to such groups was based on the need for the services offered. Humanitarian and government programs can make a more grounded impact if they worked with the local organizations and built their capacities through providing resources like financial literacy, management, and leadership skills. Working through the community-based programs also builds community resilience by rebuilding members' esteem, unity, and sense of belonging. It is also important to understand local power structures and groups of influence. Programs should thus be tailored to suit local circumstances and conditions. It also is important to understand how affected communities conceptualize vulnerability and marginalization, and include it in assistance distribution. The process of recovery is thus most productive when advanced from a community development perspective and efficient when conducted at the local level with the active participation of the affected community and considering local capacities and expertise for sustainability.

It is also critical in reconstruction phases for programs to target those groups of the population, which constitute a higher risk for conflict re-eruption and general instability within the community. In northern Uganda these are the youth, yet their concerns have not been centered around peacebuilding. Young people constitute a large portion of the population and recently have been involved with armed and violent groups. It is imperative that reconstruction programs avail youth with positive options or else they risk the youth rejoining the violent groups in the region, or continuing their violent lifestyle in the resettlement areas because they look at violence as a normal way of life. In post-conflict settings, youth need to be economically involved and also socially included in activities and locations that motivate them. Previous research has demonstrated that youth can serve as agents of peace both during and after armed conflicts (UNDP 2007; Schwartz 2010; Sommers 2007). Social involvement can be in the form of youth workshops to share experiences and skills in trade, HIV prevention, and treatment and peacebuilding. This study confirmed too, that the young generation appreciates peace as evidenced through the strategies (like naming) they adopted on return. Youth therefore double as high risk for violence and high potential for peace hence the need to positively direct their energy.

The foregoing discussion has focused on the individual, interpersonal, and community group levels. I now switch to a wider analysis of systems and institutions. This is not to mean that these boundaries are solid. Strategies filtrate across institutional and structural challenges and so do recommendations and conclusions.

Institutional and Structural Approaches

Besides community involvement, there exists as well a need to adopt multi-sectoral approaches especially in dealing with sexual and gender based violence in fragile regions like northern Uganda. For example, the legal sector, police, schools, and hospitals can work together to minimize violence against young women by providing a youth friendly environment to encourage access and use of available services and resources, for instance, contraceptive use.

Violence in northern Uganda has been institutionally and structurally grounded and reinforced by the government and institutions like police, schools, and hospitals through unfair policies and programs. It is thus critical for researchers to explore the relations between interpersonal (individual) and institutional violence if lasting peace is to be attained. I observed that the minority groups doubly experience more interpersonal violence and structural violence. Because violence against women is interconnected and interrelated at different forms and levels, it is very hard to minimize. While I have cited individual cases of abuse to elaborate on some forms of violence, I have attempted to situate such violence to show how institutions and structures reinforce each other to normalize the violence women and girls experience. Approaches to end violence must be generalizable yet at the same time specific to accommodate the various facets of social life including class, gender, motherhood, and marital status.

Peacebuilding in northern Uganda demands structural transformation. Using the case of northern Uganda, I agree with other feminist conflict scholars that war is a system and not an event that happens on the battlefield (Butler 2010; Sjoberg 2014). This is because the effects of war, including trauma, violence, food insecurity and disease, continue well into the post-conflict stage (Wibben 2011). War affects everyone in the community including children, mothers, wives, elders, men, and leaders. In my study, each of these groups had a role to play in the violence young women experienced. Some children, for instance, were involved as soldiers and participated in rape and other forms of sexual assault against women. Theories that focus on individuals as the central factor in causing violence like the youth bulge theory point to young men, undermine this understanding of war as a system (Butler 2010) that individuals may not be able to control. Individualized approaches also downplay the role of institutions and structures in causing violence (Sjoberg 2013; Tripp et al. 2013). Disregarding such complexities affects peacebuilding processes.

For sustainable reintegration, it is paramount that program implementation in northern Uganda be built on openness and transparency especially toward the local population. This can be achieved through open public dialogues about policies in locally understood language and accessible venues. Since the central and local governments set the guidelines for NGOs operation in northern Uganda, openness and accountability can be incorporated as a requirement for humanitarian agencies operating in the region and communities can be involved in evaluation of humanitarian practices in relation to open public discussions. I argue that this is a good strategy because, open discussions can minimize corruption and poor management of programs yet at the same time will focus on the needs of the community. It can also generate hope for the communities and thus trigger their thinking about the future hence support long-term development projects including education.

Beyond the national level, reliance on country-specific strategies halts efforts to solve complex and protracted war situations like the situation in northern Uganda. The war in northern Uganda escalated beyond borders to include neighboring countries like Sudan, Democratic Republic of Congo and Central African Republic (CAR). I thus recommend that the affected nation state governments work together to come up with regional initiatives to curb the LRA. Each affected state can choose members to form a regional committee to discuss peace with both rebels and local communities. This committee should intentionally include women and feminists as members. In northern Uganda women like Sr. Rachel[1] already have demonstrated that women can be great peacebuilders. Having feminist representation on the committee would encourage representation of women's concerns and needs during and after conflict. War as a system has become a regional issue for which nation-centered frameworks do not provide desired results. It is now time to use peaceful regional approaches that bring together various views stretching beyond peace and conflict studies, to other relevant approaches including feminism in ending violence.

Armed violence creates suffering. However, such experiences also generate spaces of gendered agency and resilience. Despite contradiction and challenges, women in northern Uganda have taken on new empowering roles. They have come up with strategies to deal with their situation; for instance, they formed groups in which they share their experiences and counsel each other Reconstruction programs need to strategically support women's new roles and positions by providing training for instance on saving and investment, marketing of produce and improved methods of agricultural production. Support can also be in the form of community sensitization to change negative attitudes challenging women's empowerment especially from conservative social frameworks that evoke pre-conflict male dominance. Elaborating on the positive impact of having empowered women can help shape community attitudes for the better.

Final Word

All in all, solving conflict starts with understanding the root causes of conflict, which for northern Uganda include unbalanced regional development and structural injustices rooted in the colonial era, but also tribalism and the struggle for power. Peacebuilding, therefore, needs to

---

[1] After the LRA rebels had abducted 139 girls from St. Mary's college, Aboke, Sister Rachele Fassera, the school's deputy headmistress, bravely followed the rebels into the bush, begging them to release the children and offered to take their place. Her courageous actions helped bring public attention to the Lord's Resistance Army's (LRA) practice of attacking schools and abducting children. https://www.hrw.org/news/2016/10/07/remembering-wisdom-ugandas-aboke-girls-20-years-later.

stretch beyond the war to include structural and historical hindrances to regional development and to address the material effects created by the historical events and processes like colonization. Armed violence is a complex multidimensional process. Its causes and consequences are multifaceted reaching spaces that are traditionally understood to be peaceful. It cuts across various levels including personal and group differences, domestic, and public spheres as well as local, national, and international frameworks. Armed violence gets even more complex when analyzed using age and gender as critical analytical categories. This research challenges conventional gendered constructions of armed violence and the dominant understandings of childhood. Understanding armed violence requires analysis of local history, identities, social institutions, and political and economic relations for the particular areas under study. This is because identities are multiple, fluid, and contextual.

Addressing recurrent crises and building resilience requires an integrated systems approach to humanitarian responses and development programs. The relationship between gender, poverty and vulnerability is complicated further by age and location. Gender roles have impacted women's access to and use of resources including land and other economic activities. Institutions like marriage work to concretize women's marginalized position by giving men exclusive rights over women's sexuality, earnings, and freedom of association and movement.

In closing, I wish to emphasize that while I have discussed the strategies paying attention to specific phases of conflict and levels, no definite boundaries can be drawn between conflict and peace. This also applies to the strategies women used in both stages, as well as in individual and public places. Women in both settings at times used similar strategies, for instance, pretense and silence were common for both women relating with their husbands and those in captivity.

REFERENCES

Brainard, L., & Chollet, D. (Eds.). (2007). *Too poor for peace? Global poverty, conflict, and security in the 21st century.* Washington, DC: Brookings Institution.

Bricker, M. (2009). Girl soldiers: The cost of survival in northern Uganda. Women News Network. *Alternet.*

Butler, J. (2010). *Frames of war: When is life grievable?* London and New York: Verso.

Collier, P. (2000). Economic causes of civil conflict and their implications for policy. *WorldBank, 23*. Washington, DC.

Dill, B., & Zambrana, R. (2009). *Emerging intersections: Race, class and gender in theory, policy and practice*. New Brunswick, NJ: Rutgers, the State University.

Dolan, C. (2009). *Social torture: The case of northern Uganda, 1986–2006*. New York and Oxford: Berghahn Books.

Machel, G. (2000, September). *The impact of armed conflict on children: A critical review of progress made and obstacles encountered in increasing protection for war affected children*. The International Conference on War Affected Children, Winnipeg, Canada.

Puechguirbal, N. (2012). The cost of ignoring gender in conflict and post-conflict situations: A feminist perspective. *Amsterdam Law Forum, 4*(1), 4–19.

Schwartz, S. (2010). *Youth in post conflict reconstruction-agents of change*. Washington, DC: United States Institute of Peace.

Sjoberg, L. (2013). *Gendering global conflict: Toward a feminist theory of war*. New York: Columbia University Press.

Sjoberg, L. (2014). *Gender, war and conflict*. Cambridge: Polity Press.

Sommers, M. (2007). Embracing the margins: Working with youth amid war & insecurity. In L. Brainard & D. Chollet (Eds.), *Too poor for peace? Global poverty, conflict, and security in the 21st century*. Washington, DC: Brookings Institution.

Soto, R. (2009). *Tall grass: Stories of suffering and peace in northern Uganda*. East Lansing: Michigan State University Press.

Tim, A., & Vlassenroot, K. (2010). *The Lord's resistance army: Myth and reality*. London: Zed Books.

Tripp, A. M., Ferree, M. M., & Ewig, C. (2013). *Gender, violence, and human security: Critical feminist perspectives*. New York: New York University Press.

UNDP. (2007). *The youth of Africa: A threat to security or a force for peace?* Conference Background Paper. http://www.genevadeclaration.org.

United Nations. (1989). *Convention on the rights of the child*. Retrieved from http://www.childrensrights.ie/sites/default/files/UNCRCEnglish.pdf.

Wibben, A. (2011). *Feminist security studies: A narrative approach*. London and New York: Routledge.

Index

A

Africa, 8, 10, 12–14, 27, 29, 33–36, 40–43, 52, 57, 61, 62, 64, 67, 69, 71–74, 76, 92, 96, 97, 101–103

Agency, 3, 40, 42, 54–56, 60, 82, 86, 97, 100, 101, 114, 139–141, 148, 154, 155, 157, 165

Armed violence, 1–3, 5, 7, 8, 10, 12, 15, 32, 33, 40, 42, 47, 53, 95, 100, 101, 107, 108, 118, 133, 157, 158, 165, 166

C

Childhood, 1–3, 5–7, 13, 18, 27–47, 51–54, 56–66, 68, 69, 71–73, 75, 76, 83–85, 87, 91, 103, 158, 166

Child labor, 29, 31, 33, 35–38, 44, 55, 56, 65–69, 71, 72, 97

Culture, 19, 28, 34, 35, 39, 53, 74, 76, 86, 90, 115, 150

D

Development, 2, 6, 11, 13, 17, 20, 29, 32, 38–40, 43, 44, 53, 57, 61, 63, 66, 68, 75, 76, 83, 85, 88, 90, 92–94, 97–99, 111, 113, 119, 139, 151, 158, 161, 162, 164–166

F

Feminism, 21, 165

Forced displacement, 8, 9, 16, 32, 33, 37, 42, 101, 139

G

Gender, 9, 10, 12, 18–21, 33, 34, 38, 56, 63–65, 68, 73, 76, 81, 85, 92–94, 96, 99, 100, 109, 117–121, 127, 131, 133, 134, 144, 147, 148, 150, 152, 154, 156, 158, 162–164, 166

Girlhood, 107, 118
Global south, 1, 5, 6, 18, 27, 32, 34, 52, 56, 94

H
Humanitarian assistance, 3, 5–7, 9, 11, 28, 37, 39, 44–46, 52, 76, 81, 84, 107–113, 116, 123, 125, 127, 129, 131–133, 147, 152, 161
Human rights, 6–8, 11, 15, 16, 28, 31–35, 37, 39, 40, 43, 46, 95, 99, 108, 119, 121, 158

I
Identity, 1, 3, 5, 6, 10, 20, 21, 31, 34, 35, 39, 47, 59, 63, 64, 67, 69, 74, 76, 82, 85, 91, 94, 140, 143, 144, 151, 153
Indigenous, 1, 6, 21, 28, 33, 36, 46, 52, 54, 63, 67, 72, 75, 94, 101, 126, 154
Intersectionality, 19, 20, 101

L
Lord's resistance army, 7, 9, 13, 133, 141, 165

P
Post-conflict, 2, 3, 6, 14, 16–18, 20, 39, 45, 52–54, 63–65, 74, 76, 81, 83, 84, 100, 103, 109–111, 119, 120, 123, 126, 127, 129, 131, 132, 134, 139, 140, 144, 146–148, 154–156, 160, 162–164

R
Recovery, 17, 53, 85, 110, 111, 113, 116, 121, 133, 151, 155, 162
Resilience, 3, 42, 55, 86, 97, 100, 101, 114, 139–141, 148, 157, 162, 165, 166

U
Uganda, 1–3, 5–10, 12–22, 27, 28, 32, 33, 35–40, 43–47, 51–58, 61–69, 71–76, 82, 83, 88, 94–98, 107–116, 118–121, 124–126, 129–134, 139, 141–144, 147–150, 152, 154, 157–165

V
Violence, 3, 7–22, 31, 36, 37, 41, 43, 62–64, 70, 71, 73, 83, 92–100, 102, 107–110, 113, 117–123, 125–129, 131, 133, 134, 144–146, 153, 157, 158, 160, 162–165
Vulnerability, 30–32, 37, 40, 56, 60, 69–71, 108, 111, 121, 154, 160, 162, 166

Y
Youthhood, 2, 3, 6, 18, 28, 46, 47, 52, 53, 57, 75, 76, 81, 83–85, 87, 88, 90–92, 94, 103

The manufacturer's authorised representative in the EU is Springer Nature Customer Service Centre GmbH, Europaplatz 3, 69115 Heidelberg, Germany. If you have any concerns regarding our products, please contact ProductSafety@springernature.com

Printed and bound by CPI Group (UK) Ltd, Croydon, CR0 4YY
23/03/2026
02076674-0002